When Will She

Stories and poems about a journey through childhood sexual, physical, and mental abuse and coming out on the other side

Written by Patricia G. Croom

I've always said I'd write a book. I've had a million thoughts about the subject matter; a fictional novel, a book of poetry, a group of short stories. I've always written. I've journaled, written poetry, written stories but never quite got down to doing it because it never felt quite right. Don't get me wrong I'd write a few things and think this might be it... only to lose the drive because it just didn't feel right. This time things felt different.

I woke up in the middle of the night several days after a conversation with my husband when he said I should write a book. I woke up with the name and the format of this book in my head. I didn't write it down, certainly I'd remember it because it was so good. I woke up later panicking because I didn't remember it. Thankfully, once I just sat with myself for a bit it all came flooding back.

This book is me sharing pieces of me and being vulnerable. It will be short stories, thoughts about life, trauma, and healing, and it will be poetry. I hope not to disappoint but the truth is my story is exclusive to me in that my perspectives are my own and might not sit or resonate well with some people. My hope, though, is that the stories and poems contained here will fill someone with hope, or help someone to overcome, or ease someone's suffering in ways that make my suffering have a meaning beyond simply suffering through childhood trauma. This book is also a journey for me; a journey in healing and to better places.

The content within is heavy reading. It's not pretty. It's the rough, the real, the damaged soul of a girl who has been fighting for years to be better. This story, when it concludes on its final page, is not the final destination, but rather a stopping point. I fully believe that we are on a lifelong journey of learning and of finding new perspectives. Life is a beautiful adventure; filled with joy, hardships, traumas, and uncertainty. Embrace what is yours, become powerful in acknowledging what you have overcome, never get too stuck in the past otherwise it will keep you from your future and always, ALWAYS continue on!

I hope that this book can give hope that there is healing, that the journey is worth it and you should stick around for it, and that you are worthy of love and all the good things that life has to offer!

Several years ago my son was dating a girl who had been abused as a child and had been adopted. There was a lot happening with this girl and her adoptive mom asked one day after finding out about my own childhood abuse "You seem fine and she's such a mess. When will she be better?"

I am not going to lie. I wanted to shake her. I wanted to shake her for her ignorance. I wanted to shake her for all the times I had been misunderstood or not seen and heard and I was fairly certain her daughter might have the same urge. She had been trying to tell me about how this teenager she had adopted was damaged, how she was a liar, how she was manipulative, how she couldn't be trusted. She told me how the girl had been abused before she had come into her home and had been in therapy for years but still wasn't better. This was when I told her about my own childhood abuse; not the full story but a general summary. She sat staring at me, shocked. Then she asked the question that became the title of this book and seemed so very fitting for a book about my life.

I suppose every parent wants their child to be better or the best version of themselves.. They want the innocent child they knew before the trauma changed them. They want a fix that puts the trauma in a box and sends it packing forever. They want the poor coping skills to go away and often they want things to go back to how they were before the trauma occurred. I stared at this woman for a moment before shaking my head and saying "she will always be trying to get better." I saw the puzzled look on her face and the disappointment and she said "But, you are fine. How did you get better?"

I shook my head "If you would have asked me as a teenager, after my mom found out about my abuse and moved, I'd have told you I was fine. I was better. When I was in my twenties I looked back at that teenage girl I had been; angry, always ready to fight, always ready to lie my way out of a situation, always wanting to be loved but pushing everyone away and I thought *'damn, girl you were a mess. Good thing you are better now.'* Then I got into my thirties and realized that the girl I had been in my twenties had still been a mess. Trying to raise children, trying to navigate a marriage, that was a lot for someone who wasn't even sure who she was. I had sleepless nights because a nightmare about my abuser would wake me and my heart would be pouding, tears running down my face, and I'd be sure he was in the house. It was really a good thing I had it together once I reached my thirties. Then I hit my forties and watched my kids leaving home, went back to school, and found my stride. I looked back at my thirties and realized I was still a bit of a mess but had come a long way. In that moment I realized that I kept working on healing but that I was always a bit of a disaster, because I thought healed meant I'd be better. Better meant carefree and happy the way I had been before the abuse started. The truth is...we are always getting better, if we are putting in the work, but we are never immune to the effects of our past trauma. Better does not mean *"as I was before."*

I could see the disappointment on her face. She didn't get it. She didn't understand trauma. I wondered why agencies like DCFS and the court system allowed people who had no clue about trauma and how it affects a child to care for children who had been through so much trauma. My heart broke for this young girl who was becoming a woman but hadn't ever known healing love and wasn't given the tools to figure it out. My heart broke because I realized her suffering would continue until she found a way to heal herself since every adult in her life was failing her. I hurt for her because her trauma continued to be added to by adults who didn't know better, but it seemed were also unwilling to learn to be better.

Childhood trauma isn't the same as a cold that comes along to invade the body and then leaves after running its course and we are better with no long term effects from the cold. This is TRAUMA. It's ugly, it is hard, it sucks and it is with you forever. It is able to creep up and trigger you when you least expect it. Trauma isn't an illness that when it's over disappears. Trauma is a lifelong partner; it walks beside you, sometimes silently, but it is there and it will bring you to your knees from time to time, out of the blue, to remind you that it can. That doesn't mean you are unhealed. Healing means you can acknowledge your trauma. You can recognize it for what it is. You can stop the self-sabotaging behaviors that served you when you needed to survive the trauma you were living but no longer serve you today. Healing means you start thriving. Healing means your breath may be taken away momentarily, but now it doesn't leave you lost, spiraling out of control. Healing means you know how to work through those moments.

I believe that each of us has a story or two inside of us. Each of us is an artist in some way or another; our experiences and feelings shaping us and triggering something in us that our art helps us work through, engage with, and grow from.

For me, that art comes in several forms; mainly writing. I'm not a novelist - I write poetry. My poetry is dark, painful, triggering at times, most times it is simple, a few lines or paragraphs. I feel the need to indicate this, because my poetry comes from a place of deep seeded pain and a lifetime of healing from childhood physical, emotional, mental, and sexual abuse, and it could trigger those who might read it.

My poetry, while dark, is a way for me to express and process my feelings, my thoughts, my insecurities and my pain. We each cope in different ways; some healthy and some unhealthy. For me poetry has been a way to cope, to scream, to yell, to throw my middle finger in the air at the man who mentally, physically, verbally, and sexually assaulted me for the entirety of my elementary and junior high years.

I have been one of the lucky ones; I escaped my hell, I was surrounded by support and love. I didn't always appreciate it, trust it, or want it. I lashed out. I was a terrible teenager; better to hurt someone than to be hurt by them. I tested every person who said they loved me...how much would they take before they walked away and left me. I expected to be alone. I believed I deserved to be unloved and at the same time I desperately wanted to be loved. I pushed everyone and yet they remained; those select few who still walk with me today, have truly been my saving grace. I wanted to love and be loved and not be all the things the insidious whispers in my head said I was...but, I pushed everyone; some saw the real me, the hurt girl that was terrified to trust love, and they not only stayed but lifted me up. I have been very lucky in this, and I know many others who were not so blessed.

We each face some type of trauma, some kind of pain. We all learn to deal with that trauma in our own ways. Research shows how trauma, especially childhood trauma, affects the brain, changing our way of thinking and coping and reasoning. Despite a long list of bad decisions that many sexual abuse survivors have made, healing is always possible. A life of joy, mindfulness, gratitude, fulfillment, and love is not out of reach; you just have to retrain your brain and then embrace all the good things you most certainly deserve!

Warrior

The past so distant - pushed back
Hidden deep within my brain

Always waiting for an opportunity to steal my peace
And leave a wasteland of self doubt and pain

As the years go by I become a stranger
The reminders of my past slip a little further away

Hundreds of miles separate me from my abuser
Thirty years have gone by

Thirty years of working on myself
Thirty years of the voice in my head telling me

'You'll never be good enough'
'You're just a worthless whore'

Thirty years of surviving
Thirty years of never giving up

My past will not define me
I'll fight it till my dying breath

Moments, events, and triggers may shake me
But my path, my course, has been set

I am the mindful warrior
Focusing on joy and healing over time

I am the confident warrior
Always reminding myself of my worth

I am the vigilant warrior
Always working on a better me.

I was born into a Portuguese family, as in recently immigrated, thick accents, lots of loud women. My mom came to the United States while pregnant with me and moved in with my aunt and uncle, who were my godparents when I was baptized. My aunt and uncle had 6 children, but opened their home to my mother and I. We only lived with them a short time. I have some memories of our time there but very few as I was so young.

My next solid and vivid memories begin when we lived in Illinois. My mom and I lived in a small house with my Avo' (grandmother, in Portuguese). This is when most of my memories begin. Another of my aunt and uncle's lived in Illinois and we saw them often. My mom actually worked at their restaurant as a waitress and she worked the 2nd shift at a factory a town or two over from the town we lived in. My Avo' was my babysitter.

This was a happy time in my life. I was loved. I knew I was loved. I spoke Portuguese and English. I often translated for my Avo who knew just a few words of English. She and one of our neighbors would often talk while I played with the neighbor's grandson. When I say they talked I should clarify; they communicated. They would speak in their own languages, but would make gestures and point and smile… I don't know if they really understood each other. I just knew everyone was happy.

One of my favorite memories is falling asleep in my avo's lap and then waking up in my mom's bed. I'd wake when my mom arrived home and went into the bathroom that was off the bedroom. She'd flip on the light and turn on the radio. The sounds would be soft, and she'd hum. I'd lay there watching her until she noticed that my eyes were open. She would sometimes pick me up and dance with me before laying me down and giving me a kiss to go back to sleep.

This was love. Good, pure, solid love.

Other memories from that time include aunts and uncles being at the house and all the women in the kitchen cooking, laughing, talking. My aunt puffing cigarettes while everyone else cooked. I had cousins, all older than me, who would play, laugh, and teach me things. Life, at that time, was joy and laughter, and love.

I often think back to those times and think that foundation is what saved me. I know this to be true. I've since read research that would indicate that the first months and years give the foundation more solidly than we once realized. I think that the abuse I later suffered wasn't able to fully break me because I had a foundation of love. I knew what love was, what it looked like, how it felt, and I knew that it was real. When you have known love, you can always reach back and hold onto that feeling, that knowledge, and carry on through some pretty terrible things.

After some time, my mom was set up on a date by another server at the restaurant. The other server had a son who was a farmer and set up a date with him and my mother. I remember him coming to the door. He was all smiles, but I was terrified of him. He was over 6 feet tall. I didn't like him. The feeling was immediate. After my mom left with him I told my Avo' that I didn't like him and that his eyes scared me. She told me that she also didn't like him but that my mom was allowed to have some fun. My response to him was something I can't explain. I knew something was not good about him. I had uncles, uncles who were big men and were forces to be reckoned with, but this man was different, he didn't feel kind.

This is the man who my mom married. This was the man who became my abuser.

Little Bitch

I didn't like you from the start
It seemed obvious there was something
Terribly wrong with your heart
But I was just a little girl no one was going to listen to

On your wedding day to my mom
I was so sad and so unsure
You took that chance to let me know
There was no comfort, and I should be scared

"Why are you crying, you little bitch?
I'll straighten you out now that I'm going to be your dad
Shut your mouth or I'll shut you up."
As you grabbed my arm and pulled me near

Hot breath on my face
The spit coming from your mouth
The look in your eyes and your sharp words let me know
I'd be living a nightmare.

My stepfather married my mom in a small church wedding in a small central Illinois town. I didn't like him. His smile never reached his eyes. His eyes scared me. They had from the moment I met him. Isn't it strange that little children can know these things while adults are fooled by words, pretty faces, smiles, and gestures?

He had tried to play with me, put me on his shoulders while he and my mom dated. I tried to be good. I tried to like him. I wanted to like him...but I just knew something was wrong. There was a feeling I couldn't shake even though I was just a little girl. My Avo' tried to comfort me that day but at one point I was crying and my avo' took me outside. He walked out, sending my avo' inside to check on my mom. He didn't kneel down to talk to me on my level but instead grabbed me and pulled me close to him asking why I was crying. He called me a little bitch. I wasn't sure what that meant. He told me to stop crying or he'd shut me up. I didn't quite understand but tried to stop my tears. My body was shaking but I tried to steady my breathing. I tried to stop the tears. I understood there was no love from this man. My arm hurt from where his large hand had grabbed me.

His father was a kind man. Interestingly, He didn't learn the hatred and the contempt and the abuse from his father. That seemed to come solely from his mother. The family attended the Apostolic Christian Church and there was a lot of praying that took place. His family farmed and he bought the family farm, with a share belonging to his sisters at some point in my childhood. We lived on the family farm, a 3-bedroom ranch style home in the country. There were several barns, for the chickens, for the pigs, and for the farm equipment. There was a lot of land, and we were a quarter mile from the neighbors. Do you know how much you can yell, and no one will hear you when people live a quarter mile away? It seemed like no one could hear him, or maybe they did but kept to themselves.

My brother was born on June 28, 1979. He was cute and precious. New babies are times of joy, right? Not in our house. The baby seemed to make my stepfather meaner. There had already been times where they'd fight and yell, but I only heard those things from my room. I'd hear my mother crying. I'd see him being nice the next day. I wasn't sure what was happening. I understood loud families, but there was always laughter before my mom married him, now there was just shouting, fear, and tears.

One night I awoke to yelling and screaming. I walked out of my room and into the hallway. I followed the noise to the kitchen and walked in to see my mom holding my baby brother and my stepfather standing over my mom screaming at her, I watched as he slapped her and said "If you weren't holding my son I'd fucking kill you." I didn't understand what was happening, but my mom was crying, my brother was screaming. I ran over and grabbed his arm as I was afraid he was going to hit her again. He threw me off him. I hit the wall, my head thudding against the tile. Everything faded to black. When I awoke, I was in my bed. My head hurt and I didn't feel good. What was happening? Why was this happening?

Fists

A little girl
Who knew only love
Thrown into a world
Where pain and fear were her only companions

Shouting and yelling
Screams and pleads
How did this happen
What could it mean

Little bitch, little bitch
Those words were new
She'd never been called bad names
What had she done wrong

Fear gripping her
It made her body rebel
Shaking and crying
Her mind so unsure

No hope for relief
But where was God
He was supposed to love her
That's what the song said

Pain from the blows to her head
Left her wondering if she'd die
No one was there to save her
What had she done wrong

She must have been very bad
But she couldn't remember when

She wasn't worth loving she heard him say
The voice echoed those words in her head every day

No one loves you, you little bitch
You're nothing but a stupid little whore
She didn't know what that meant
But it must have been very bad

The fists rained down on her tiny body
Bruises and blood
Tears and pleads
He let her know she was no good

She looked with eyes filled with tears
Trying to understand what thing she had done
She didn't know and no one would tell her
Just the words and the fists that created her understanding

She was sure she would break
He was so big and she so small
The next hit might be the end
Please let me die she prayed

My stepfather's mother never liked me. It seemed that no matter what I did I made her angry. She had a grandson who had been adopted and was a year or two older than me. If he wanted a toy I was playing with she'd grab it from me and sometimes pinch me until tears came to my eyes for playing with it and not giving it to him when he wanted it. He'd often not even ask but instead go to her and "tell on me" for not sharing. When I'd go to visit, she'd get Dairy Queen but tell me to eat leftovers from her fridge.

The town she lived in had a fair every fall. I remember being there with my mom and stepdad. I was sent with my stepfather's mom and dad to go to the VFW hall for a show. The room was packed and to my 5-year-old self, the room seemed much larger than it did in later years. After the show everyone stood and was talking. I thought my stepfather's dad told me to go a certain direction. I started walking, there were so many people and so much noise. I walked out the side door and onto the sidewalk and looked back...I did not see my stepfathers' parents. I kept standing there waiting but they didn't come.

I was scared. I was lost and everyone who had come out of the side door was making their way back up to the main street where all the rides and everything else were. I walked up that way but there were so many people up there and even more noise, so I walked back to the door. I waited again. Still, no one came and no one else seemed to notice me or think I might be lost. I realized that the pastor at our church lived just behind the VFW and there was a light on in the kitchen of his house. I ran there and knocked on the door, but no one came. I walked back to the door of the VFW.

Finally, my stepfather's mom and dad found me. I was crying. I was so glad to have been found. When my mom and stepfather got there my mom hugged me, she was happy to see me. Then I was asked "Why would you run away from us like that?" I had not run away. I replied to my stepfather's mother that I had thought grandpa had told me to go to that door, pointing to the side door to the hall. She looked at my stepfather and said "She is lying, you know that. She is lying and she did that just to scare everyone." I could see his face change. I knew something bad was going to happen. We left the fair. We drove home in our old red Monte Carlo. As I sat in the back seat, I could see the lights from our town getting closer and he started asking me why I had wanted to scare his mother. I replied that I had not, I had just gotten mixed up.

By the time we were home he was absolutely enraged. He was screaming. Spit was hitting me in the face when he would bend down and yell at me. He told me to go to my room and get my pajamas on. I did exactly that and climbed into my bed praying that I'd get to go to sleep. But as I lay in my bed, I could hear him yelling. He called me back to the kitchen. He asked again why I had wanted to scare his mom. I told him again that I had not. I told him I thought grandpa told me to go that way, to the side door. He called me a lying bitch. He took off his belt. He grabbed me by my arm and whipped me with the belt. He asked the question again. I answered the same way. He threw me toward the corner where the stove and the doorway to the den was and told me to stand there. He repeated his question. I answered again. He whipped me again with the belt. I was crying, I was hardly able to breathe because it hurt so badly, and I was trying not to cry so I could answer him.

He didn't believe me. Pretty soon I was told to stand with my hands over my head. He placed a Sears or Montgomery Ward catalog on my hands (if you remember the time period, those catalogs were several inches thick) and told me not to drop them. He asked me again why I had wanted to scare his mom. I told him the same answer. He whipped me again. I dropped the books, and pee ran down my legs. He picked the catalogs back up and told me to raise my hands again. I did as exactly as I was told. I began biting the inside of my mouth to keep the screams from coming out which just made him angrier.

I didn't understand. We repeated this same thing, over and over, for hours. I cannot tell you how much time went by. All I know is that by the time it was over my mom was sobbing and he had hit her a few times for raising 'a lying little bitch' like me. I tried to stand still so the catalogs wouldn't fall, he added 2 more throughout the night as he continued to question me and whip me. My body was shaking, I was standing on a wet carpet, and each blow from his belt moved my entire body, so I kept dropping the catalogs. At some point in the night, maybe he was getting tired, he told me to tell him what he knew the truth was and then went on to spell it out: I had walked away from his parents because I wanted attention and I wanted to scare everyone.. I realized in that moment that the truth to my stepfather didn't actually mean the truth they talked about at church, it meant the truth he believed and wanted to hear. I answered him with what he wanted to hear: "I wanted to scare everyone. I just wanted to go that way." He grabbed me and slapped my face. "See, that wasn't so hard. I'll teach you not to lie to me."

With that I was sent to the bathroom to clean myself up. With shaking hands, my mouth bleeding from biting it, and a bruised and battered body I went to my room on legs that felt like they couldn't take another step, but I didn't dare not succeed in what I had been told to do for fear of another beaten more. I went to my room to get fresh underwear and a new nightgown and went to the bathroom where I took a washcloth and hot soapy water and washed my soiled body. I could see bruises and welts on my legs and arms, and I wondered what my butt and back looked like. I crawled into my bed crying, burying my head in my pillow to try to hide and muffle my cries so I didn't draw his attention to me again. I didn't know what I was supposed to do. Nothing made sense. I had lied and that was a sin. They told us that in church. Sinners went to hell. I was sure I was going to hell, and I wondered how soon that would be.

LIAR

Liar, Liar, pants on fire
The children called out

I was a part of the group
Calling someone a liar

But what would they say
If they knew that I was a liar too

I lied to protect myself
I lied to live

They didn't know how
The fists felt when the blows landed

They didn't know
That the truth was overrated

Truth wasn't good
Not for me

Truth would get me beaten
Truth would make me bleed

Liar, liar, pants on fire
The children called out

Screaming at another child
Did that child know and understand

Liars were made

By Adults who didn't love them

Liar, Liar pants on fire
I guess that's me.

When I was in Kindergarten I was playing in my room. I was standing in front of the built-in drawers and mirror using an old brush that had been my stepfather's. I was brushing my hair because my stepfather's mom had told me girls are supposed to be pretty and pretty girls brush their hair at least 100 times every morning and every night.

I was lost in some daydream while I did this and didn't know my stepfather was standing in the doorway watching me. When he finally spoke it scared me, and I jumped at the sound of his deep voice and the brush flew into the air. When it landed on the wooden floor the handle broke. I looked up and saw the look in his eyes change as he stared at the brush. He reached toward me, but I ran. I ran down the hallway towards the kitchen, I ran through the kitchen and had almost made it to the den, where I would have been trapped but what does a Kindergartener know about escaping someone?

As I got close to the stove, and the doorway that often served as the corner I was to stand in when being punished, he shoved me. I fell, or maybe flew, into the door frame, my head hitting it hard. I fell to the ground. My mom screamed and ran to me. There was blood coming down the side of my face. It seemed to be a lot of blood. I was not sure why. My mom ran to the bathroom and grabbed a towel to wrap my head in and then grabbed the keys to the car. My stepfather walked over to her and grabbed her wrist forcing her to drop them. "Let the little bitch bleed." He said this after pulling her close to him and I could see the spit from his mouth hitting my mom in the face. She was crying.

He dropped her arm, and she ran back to me. Holding me to her and rocking and whispering to me that I was going to be okay. The blood soaked through the towel and was staining my mom's shirt. She began pleading with him that I had to get to the hospital because I was going to bleed to death otherwise. He finally grabbed the keys, and they took me to the hospital. I have no memory of the 12-mile ride. Everything was black. I remember thinking before I lost consciousness that I'd never grow up and get to be a pretty girl or a smart girl, I'd never get married and have babies of my own.

I awoke to bright lights, doctors, nurses, and a very cold room. I was shivering and a nurse was rubbing my shoulder and arm and gave me a warm blanket. As the doctors shaved a part of my head and gave me stitches, they asked what had happened. I didn't say anything. My stepfather supplied the answers. He indicated that we were playing in the house, and he tried to tag me but did it too hard and I fell over and hit the door frame. The doctor paused the stitching of my head and got down to look me in the eyes and asked if that was true. I thought this doctor had kind eyes, but I knew my stepfather would kill him, or at the very least kill me if I didn't agree with his story. I tried to nod my head in agreement. That really hurt. Tears were coming out of my eyes. No wonder God didn't love me. I was just a big liar.

I have looked back sometimes to moments like these in my memories and wondered if I had spoken my truth would it have saved me years of pain? The truth is I don't know what would have happened. What I do know is even the kindest and most caring people recognized the abuse for what it was or at least had an inkling that there was abuse and still didn't step in to save me and even if I had spoken up the laws weren't there to save me. I may have ended up with far more dire consequences than I did. One can never predict what might have been and dwelling on it serves no purpose other than to take us down a path that does not change the outcome through which we have already lived.

Comply

You ask for the truth
But it's not what you want.

It's the lies, it's the version
That you are convinced of.

The version that fits the scenario you created
No other version or actual truth will satisfy.

If I'm asked for a truth
I know I have to lie

I protect you, but I hate you
I wish you would die

But I know to comply
With the versions you share

My own death sentence
Is at your will if I answer any other way

I don't think people believe the lies
I wait for them to point out the truth or to try to save me

But the lies are easier
Than facing the horror that's real

So, I repeat your lies and they all nod
I will comply.

My Avo lived with us for a time on the farm. Things were calm for a short time. She and I shared a room. She was full of joy and love. I can still see her smile and hear her laughter if I just close my eyes and think about her.

She didn't speak English, or rather her English was just a handful or two of words. She spoke Portuguese. My stepfather hated that. It made him insanely crazy because he did not know what we were saying, and he was afraid we were talking about him.

One morning we woke to the sound of him yelling. I jumped out of my bed to see what he was yelling at my mom about, but Avo told me to come back to my bed. She came over to my bed and we sat talking, I am sure she was trying to distract me. I could still hear the yelling, and it was getting louder. I knew something bad was going to happen and I jumped up and ran to the kitchen where the noise was coming from. Avo followed me.

We arrived in the kitchen just in time to see him slap my mother. My Avo jumped in, yelling, pleading in Portuguese for him to stop and using the few English words she knew. This enraged him. He slapped my Avo. I felt like I had been kicked in the stomach. How could he do that? What had she done? She wanted to protect her daughter. She was good. She was not bad like me or bad like him.

He began screaming. He wanted her out of his house. "Get out of my house. You aren't welcome here anymore. You raised a stupid whore for a daughter." Spit was streaming out of his mouth as he screamed.

My Avo turned and walked to the room we shared. I stood there staring, shocked, I didn't know what to do. I needed to make sure my mom was okay, but my Avo had just been slapped by this huge man. I ran to my room. My avo had a suitcase out and was packing her things. I pushed her things away, I grabbed her, throwing my arms around her waist. I told her I was going with her and that I did not want to be there anymore. She promised me that if she left things would be better. She told me I had to stay with my mom. She hugged me, she was crying. I was crying. I didn't care, I wasn't staying and if my mom wanted to she would stay without me because I was going with my Avo. She sat on the bed with a sigh and pulled me into her lap; rocking me, hugging me, and whispering that it would be better if she wasn't there. I knew this wasn't true. I tried to tell her. She sat with me for a long time. I fell asleep in her arms.

She went to live with my aunt and uncle. I was angry. I was sad. I felt abandoned. No one seemed to understand that things would never be okay if we were there! I hated my stepfather for making my avo' leave. I hated him for all the terrible things he did, but nothing I could do would stop it and I could not let him know that I hated him. I was sure there would be no safety for me if he knew how I felt about him.

Alone

The big room
Wasn't far enough away
To drown out the sounds
Of his anger and the cut of his words

There was no safe place
In this home
There was no safe person
To protect a small child

Everyone just trying to survive
A madman's anger
A word, a look could send the day
Into tears, and screams, and pleads for mercy

The child quickly learns
There is no reprieve
And that she is
Completely alone in this world.

I rode the bus. It's interesting, riding the bus. Our school was small. Elementary students, junior high kids, and high schoolers were all on the same bus. The older groups were so cool, seeming confident and happy. You can learn a lot on the bus, if you pay attention to what everyone else is talking about.

There was a girl a year older than me who lived down the road, a mile from my house. She was nice and we often sat together on the bus. She was complaining one day about her dad being mean. I misunderstood. I thought of 'being mean' to be like my stepfather. I told her about him hitting me. She looked horrified and I understood I'd made a mistake, so I asked her not to tell anyone.

That night we sat at dinner. We had not taken more than a few bites when there was the sound of tires on gravel and then a knock on the door. We weren't expecting anyone, but my mom got up and answered the door. She came back to the table and told my stepfather that the neighbor was at the door for him. I could hear them talking, I knew they were talking about me and what I had told his daughter. I was afraid but as my heart raced, I thought maybe he was so upset to hear what my stepfather had done to me that he had come to make him stop. These were just the naive hopes of a young girl, instead before leaving he told my stepfather to keep me in line and to make sure I understood that family business shouldn't be shared. My heart sank and I already knew what was coming.

The door shut and my stepfather watched, waved, and smiled as the neighbor got into his truck and pulled out onto the road then he turned. His smile was gone. I could see that he was angry. "What did you tell his daughter?" he screamed with his finger against my nose. "What the fuck did you tell his daughter?"

Words wouldn't form properly. "I, I, I ...I don't know. Nothing." We both knew that was a lie but what was I supposed to say? He didn't even bother to ask again. He grabbed me from my chair, reaching under my arm and grabbing me under the armpit, yanking me away from the table. My chair went flying out and knocked over. Spit was flying out of his mouth as he dragged me to the living room, still holding me under the arm and unhooking his belt, yanking it off. He began spanking me. "You don't tell anyone what happens in this fucking house, do you understand me you little bitch? You're a good for nothing whore. Shut that fucking mouth of yours." He went on and on. I was blinded by tears and by the spit when he would turn me to scream in my face before yanking me back around to whip me some more. His anger rarely subsided quickly.

He was angry. I'd embarrassed him, he said. The neighbor had told him that his daughter didn't need to know about those things, and he'd better get me in line to keep our family business to myself. He continued beating me. He must have gotten tired. He told me to get cleaned up and go to my room. On wobbly legs I took myself to my room to get clean clothes and then to the bathroom to clean myself up. Tears were still streaming down my face; I was trying to keep my sobs under control because making too much noise might get his attention and make him mad all over again. I went to my room and laid on the bed on my stomach, my backside hurt so much.

That night I learned that sharing those secrets with anyone would result in nothing good for me. No one cared, no one would make him stop. I was in 1st grade, and I had no hope, no faith, and no trust. I prayed anyway. If there was a God, how could I have done so many bad things when I was so little? Maybe if I said I was sorry he would make it stop.

I also knew that wasn't how things would work. I prayed for God to make me die. At least if I died this terrible pain would stop. I had only told her a small bit of information, not even going into the really serious things before realizing my mistake. The look of horror on her face let me know I shouldn't have told her anything. I don't know why I had told her anything in the first place, my house wasn't like other people's homes, and I knew that.

Who Knew?

The truth is they all knew
They had ideas about what happened behind closed
doors.

The days missed from school
The random bruises met with downcast eyes

They knew but did nothing and the rage filled my soul
Why didn't they help me?

It was a different time, outsiders didn't make waves
Silent thoughts and maybe some prayers

All just watched but no one would intervene
We all knew our role and we all knew our place

To speak to a friend was met with an angry visit from her
dad
Telling him the secrets I had shared

The words still echo in my head
"Keep her in line, my daughter doesn't need to hear those
things"

The fear crept in before he even turned to leave
That fear was a song beating through my body; almost
electric

Buzzing and thundering in my head
My body began shaking before the first blow was felt

No savior would protect me, no father would intervene

The lesson learned at such a young age.

The beating was swift and it was severe
Fists and slaps landed, the belt 'thwapped' against my
skin.

My body lay in a heap, bruises forming
While my spirit felt broken

My lesson that night driven home with a final kick
"Keep your mouth shut, you little bitch"

The signs were there, everyone knew
But it was a time when willful ignorance ruled.

A young girl learns quickly
Hold the secrets silently and fake smiles

No heroes would come, no savior would arrive
She realized she needed to adapt to survive.

My mom left on more than one occasion. I don't want her vilified in this. She did the best she could, with what tools she had. It was a time when divorce was considered bad, the woman looked at as a failure. While there were a small number of resources, they were minimal and in central Illinois they were not always readily accessible.

Once she left him shortly after my second brother was born. We went to a shelter for battered women that was located inside an old hotel that had been converted into a shelter. I remember the hallways being dimly lit. Our room was small. My baby brother slept inside a drawer to the dresser that my mom put blankets down in to make it softer. There were counselors, although at the time I did not know what they were called.

One day I was with a group of the kids that were there. We were playing tag through the halls. An older boy, he was between 10 and 12 told me he needed to get something from his room. We went to his mom's room; it was as dimly lit as all the others. He told me I could sit on the bed, and I did. We were talking while he rummaged through a drawer. When he found what he wanted he walked over to the bed and pushed me back and then climbed on top of me and started kissing me. I didn't know what was happening and I started pushing him and yelling. He got up and asked me what was wrong. I told him I didn't like what he had done. He shrugged his shoulders and said sorry. We left his room.

Years later I realized that he had likely been exposed to things he shouldn't have been and was likely just mimicking what he had seen. That may have even been why his mom had gone to the shelter in the first place.

Who knew? The incident scared me. It was unexpected, something I didn't enjoy and something I just didn't understand.

I remember pastors from our church coming out and talking about my stepfather with my mom. 'He feels really bad.' 'He has been going to the VA here to get help for his anger.' 'He loves you and didn't mean to do those things.' 'The Bible says wives submit to your husbands.' I really began to question the things the bible said then. How was it that a God we sang songs about, a God who loves and protects us would want a wife to live with a mean husband? The elders who were supposed to know everything and who all were so nice to me seemed to not know much of anything. I was 8 and knew something was terribly wrong.

This play at guilt and shame based on biblical principles and reminding my mom of what God would want disgusts me now. It is manipulation based on a gross and twisted sense of entitlement and domination that has often been used to manipulate and control. However well-intentioned the person saying these things was because much of it was ingrained in them from a lifetime of teachings, the truth was they helped create so much more harm and a very twisted and damaging understanding of God for me, and perhaps many others.

Praise Jesus

Jesus loves me this I know
For the Bible tells me so

We sing the song in Sunday School
But I don't believe it anymore

Jesus must not love me
Maybe I'm just bad like my stepdad says

Jesus does not love me
Of this I am sure

Why am I bad
I try to be so good

Jesus loves the good children
The ones that aren't me

I hide my bruises while I sing
What would they all think if they knew Jesus doesn't love
me?

Mom went back to him. I remember being so confused by that when it happened repeatedly, but I understand now, she did the best she could with the resources she had. It was also the 80's, if the cops came, they asked you right in front of the man if he had hit you, even if you were standing there with a broken nose and shattered teeth. They asked if you wanted to press charges, again with him standing there, but they didn't actually keep you safe. Domestic disputes weren't taken seriously, it was a family matter to be dealt with internally. It was a different time. Add in the church officials who talked about the biblical writings about submitting to your husband and the man being the head of the household. Child abuse was looked at with the same lens; family matters to be dealt with inside the family, especially in a small town.

She'd leave again, I think I was in the 3rd or 4th grade then. We moved into an apartment in town. I loved it there. I was close to my best friend. I was just down the road from the school. I could meet my friends as they were on their way to school. I need to stop here to explain that my school was K-8 and had about 100 kids in it. This was a small farm community in Central Illinois. Everyone knew everyone and your business was everyone's business; whispered gossip was why everyone knew everyone's business, but no action would ever be taken to make things like that right. When I came home from school one day and saw Richard's truck there I didn't understand why. Mom explained after he left that he had just been there to visit my siblings. I believed it. She meant it to be nothing more than that, but we all know that monsters find their way back even when it seems impossible.

Soon he was spending the night. I hated him. I loathed him. He promised he was going to the VA and getting counseling. My mom believed him. Maybe he was. It wasn't going to help. I knew it, why didn't she?

One morning I woke up because I fell out of bed. I must have been having a nightmare because I had my sheets tangled around my feet. I was disoriented and didn't know what was going on. He swung open the door to my bedroom demanding an answer to "What the fuck are you doing in here?" I told him I had fallen out of bed. He didn't believe or like that answer; it didn't fit with whatever scenario he had in his head. He told me I was lying. I wasn't. I looked at my mom pleadingly because I could see him ramping up and I needed help. Why didn't she make him leave? He wasn't even my dad!

He told me to make my bed, get dressed for school, and then get to the living room to talk about this some more. I understood what was happening. He was going to try a new approach; he wasn't going to beat me. He couldn't, we weren't out on the farm with the protection of no one being around. We were in town, and the neighbors might call the police. I did as I was instructed and walked into the living room. He sat on the chair and said he knew I wasn't telling the truth. He wanted to know what I was really doing. I told him again that I must have been having a nightmare because I woke up when I landed on the floor. He told me I was lying and to go stand in the corner. I stood in the corner. Seething! After a while he called me back over. A new line of questioning began. Did I not want him there? I answered honestly that I didn't. Foolishly I thought living in an apartment with so many neighbors made me safe plus mom had promised she wasn't going to go back to the farm. Why didn't I love him? He just wanted to be my dad, when obviously my own dad hadn't even wanted me. Didn't I love him when all he had ever done was try to make me better because the way I was, I'd be good for nothing except for laying on my back for a living. I didn't understand what he was talking about, but I didn't respond and I didn't ask questions.

My mom came back to the living room and told me to get to school. I grabbed my things and left the apartment feeling like a dark cloud had settled back over me. I had lived in that apartment for almost an entire school year, but I knew that was coming to an end. The world seemed to have gone very gray again. Nothing was okay.

Not long after this incident we packed our things and moved back to the farm. I moved to the bigger room on the Northeast corner of the house and my brothers took the middle room of the 3-bedroom ranch. I was in the bedroom farthest away from my mom and stepdad's and I thought that would give me some amount of reprieve. I was terribly mistaken.

I understood that life would go back to what it had been. He would start hitting me soon. I just knew it. What I didn't know was that another kind of torture would begin and that would leave a far more devastating aftermath.

Nightmares

A child wants to trust
A child wants to be good
To do what they are told they should

It's sad when a child knows
That their tears and pain
Aren't allowed to be seen

Put a smile on
It's easiest on them
This nightmare is only for you

In the darkness of the night
In the emptiness of your country home
Monsters live and breath

The nightmares occur
When you're awake or
When you're asleep

The dream feels as real as the waking horrors
There is no escape
There is no one to help

No God to come stop it
No hero will win the day
You and your nightmares are all that you have

My mom had a job at the factory in a nearby town for a while. She worked second shift. My stepfather sometimes had to cook dinner or reheat things. He also didn't care if I didn't like something. I had to eat it. One night he made fish sticks. They were still cold in the middle. I loved fish until this night.

We sat down to eat, there was corn, fish sticks, mashed potatoes, bread and butter, and milk. I began eating and after a couple bites of my fish stick realized that the middle was still cold. I tried to tell him, but he told me to be quiet and keep eating. I ate the corn, the mashed potatoes and the bread and butter. I didn't eat the other couple of fish sticks because they were still cold in the middle. He was reading some farm magazine. I asked if I could be excused from the table when I was finished. He looked up and noticed the fish sticks uneaten except for the first one I had started eating. He told me to finish the fish sticks.

I told him they were cold, and I didn't think they had been cooked all the way. I saw the change in his posture and in his face. OH NO! He reached out and slapped me. "Do you think we are made of money? Do you think you get to be picky? Your mom and your grandma spoiled you and let you get away with anything you wanted. Eat the rest of your food on your plate."

I picked up the first fish stick. I dipped it in the ketchup thinking it would help. It did not. I took a bite, trying desperately to chew and swallow. I began gagging. I took a drink of my milk and tried to breathe through my nose. "Stop acting like that and eat your goddamn food." I tried! I finally managed to swallow the bite. Tears were in my eyes.

"What the fuck are you crying about? Do you want me to give you something to cry about?" I shook my head and quickly took another bite. I was fighting back tears, trying not to gag, and trying to breathe through my nose. After a few more bites, I couldn't stop what happened next even now. I began gagging so badly that the food fell out of my mouth. Tears were streaming out of my eyes. I was trying. He stood up and pulled off his belt. He yanked me up out of my chair and hit me 3 times across the bottom of my back and my butt. He then put me back into my chair. "Eat your goddamn dinner and stop acting like a spoiled little bitch." I took another fish stick in my now shaking hands, taking a deep breath and took a bite. I tried to chew quickly and swallow. I did it. I took another bite. I repeated this, crying, breathing through my nose, praying I could do this. I couldn't. I gagged again and this time everything came back up, onto my plate.

He was furious. He was cursing and screaming and grabbed me again from my chair, hitting me with the belt some more. He then grabbed the plate, shoved it at me, and told me to wash off the plate and clean off the rest of the fish sticks because I was going to eat them. I was crying hysterically, trying to breathe, shaking like crazy from head to toe. I walked on shaky legs to the kitchen sink and rinsed off the remaining fish sticks. He told me to get back to the table. I sat back down and as told, began to try to eat them again. There was no way my body was going to eat them. I vomited again. This time on the floor of the kitchen. "You stupid, ungrateful little bitch. Clean up your mess." I went to the utility room and grabbed things to clean up the mess I'd made. When I finished cleaning it he told me to go into the living room. I knew what was coming.

I stood in the living room with my head down, tears streaming, body shaking as I tried to control my crying. I was gasping for air because I was crying so hard. He was so furious. He was pacing in front of me. Screaming at me for wasting good food. Telling me I was ungrateful. I was a little bitch. I was stupid. I was nothing but a fucking bastard, my own father hadn't even wanted me. He stopped talking and stood looking at me for a few minutes and then ordered me into the corner to stand and think about how I had acted when all I had to do was eat a perfectly good dinner.

I was still crying and shaking. He told me to raise my arms. I waited for him to grab the Sears and Montgomery Ward catalogs. This was one of his favorite punishments. I was a small child and those catalogs from the early 80's were heavy for a little kid. He stacked two on my hands. "Don't you fucking drop them." I stood concentrating on keeping my arms still. This concentration made me stop crying. That helped, without the sobs my body wasn't shaking as much. This didn't last long though because the weight of those catalogs on my small arms was too much and I began shaking. He saw this. "Don't you fucking drop those or I'll show you how bad it can get." I knew he would, and I knew I was going to drop them.

When I finally dropped them, not from lack of effort or giving up but because the weight made my arms shake so badly, he stood from his seat and put out his Pal Mal in the ashtray. He walked over to me, grabbed me by the arm and whipped me with the belt until he felt like it was enough. I counted to twenty hits before the sobs and the pain made me lose track. He threw me back into the corner. I fell to the ground "Get up, you fucking bitch. I should just kill you. You are worthless." I stood. "Raise your fucking arms."

We repeated the process for hours. I know it was hours because my mom got off work at midnight and I was still in that living room when she got home. She asked what had happened. He was not as angry now. To this day, I think he was just enjoying making sure I knew I was powerless, worthless and only because he allowed it, was I still alive. My mom talked to him and soon she told me to go to the bathroom. I went to the bathroom and peeled off my clothes.

She came in and ran a bath from me. She was crying as she washed me, looking at the bruises and welts. She kept whispering how sorry she was. She wasn't as sorry about it all as I was. If only I could be good this wouldn't happen. I tried to be good, but I didn't seem to know how. I kept thinking about him saying that he should just kill me. What would happen if I died? I'd go to hell; I was sure of that. I didn't want to go to hell. Somewhere in my mind, I knew I wasn't bad, but I also thought I was being punished for something because why would the God who saved and loved people, not want to save me?

She dried me off, put clean clothes on me and put me in my bed, kissing my forehead and telling me she loved me. I knew she did, but why did this have to be happening? Why couldn't she leave? Why did he hate me? What had I done that was so bad? I wasn't trying to be bad, why couldn't he see that? Why did my dad not want me? Where was my dad? Who was my dad?

I laid awake for a long time after with questions running through my mind that I would not find answers to for many years.

Breaking

She lay alone in her bed
Tears sliding without sound down the side of her face

She didn't understand
Her mind raced with a thousand questions

She didn't know the answers to
She didn't know it would take a lifetime to find them

Why had this happened?
How could she stop it?

There was no truth and no love
Just pain and tears and fear

Her body lay bruised and battered
Tiny and harmed in ways that should never happen

The bigger crime was that her mind was breaking
She no longer understood and was instead resigned to die

She knew it couldn't be long
So broken and battered and without any hope

If not today, it would come
Death was seeking her

A grown man of over six feet tall with closed fists
Beating her until she crumbled on the floor

Over and over again
He let her live, he told her

It was his decision and he hated her
It was just a matter of time

She wanted to die
It would bring an end to the pain

And if she did survive, would she ever be okay
Pieces of her were breaking and they might never be fixed.

Over-easy eggs, scrambled eggs, poached eggs, hard boiled eggs. There are many ways to cook and eat eggs. As a kid, over-easy eggs with their runny yolks were not something that even remotely appealed to me. I liked scrambled or hard-boiled eggs. My siblings preferred scrambled. One morning my mom made breakfast. Meals were important in our home. Farmers ate meat and potatoes for breakfast and dinner with sandwiches and such for most lunches per my stepfather. Breakfast was served and my mom realized she had made too many over-easy eggs and not enough scrambled. He told her to give me the over-easy egg. I tried to eat the other things and then claim to be full; it worked for my brother.

I asked if I could be excused to get ready for church. He said yes, and then he noticed the egg yolk (I had eaten all the rest of it) still sitting there. He told me to finish it. I sat back down, tears burning in my eyes which I tried to keep from falling. I picked at it. I asked for a piece of toast to dip in it thinking that might make it better. The way the yolk clung to it and then dripped off made my stomach do a flip-flop.

My mom tried to argue for me. She told him I had eaten enough and needed time to get ready for church. I hoped that would work. It didn't. This simple meal where no one had been yelled at suddenly turned into another nightmare.

He told her to get my siblings ready for church and leave informing her that I'd be staying behind. There was no arguing, and we all knew it. She left and he whipped me. I've described his whippings enough at this point to not need to go into detail. However, today he had a new twist. He told me to walk to the basement. I walked to the basement, down the stairs, wondering what he could be planning in the cold, cement basement. He opened a small "door" that was about three feet up the wall which I knew led to the dirt crawl spaces under the floors of the upstairs. He told me to get inside. I stood, shocked and scared, wondering why he would want me to get in there. I asked what I was supposed to do in there. He smiled… not a real smile, the smile of someone cruel "Because sooner or later you are going to understand that I can make your life easy, or I can make it hard. You will sit in there until I say you can come out." I pleaded; he slapped my face. "Get your fucking ass in there now or I'll put you in there." I walked over and pulled myself inside. I had to sit with my knees up and my upper body bent forward towards my knees otherwise my head would hit the board above me. It was so dark. There was no light. The door closed and I heard the locking mechanism click.

'What is wrong with you? Why couldn't you just eat the egg? So stupid. Why are you so stupid? This wouldn't have happened if you weren't such a stupid bitch." My mind had even turned against me because I was so stupid. I sat wondering how long he would leave me there. It was dark, and musty there. Something ran over my bare feet. I screamed. I began crying. I began begging "Please let me out. I will eat the rest of the egg. I'm sorry." He must have been standing right outside the door waiting for me to be frightened. I heard the lock unlatch and thought this was it, he would let me get out. Instead, he opened the door and told me "Shut your fucking mouth you little bitch or I swear to god this will get much worse. You will stay in there until I think you've learned your lesson." He slammed the door shut again. The dark scared me, the noises that some of the bugs made as they moved scared me. I tried to think of

other things, music, stories, things I'd read. Anything to take my mind somewhere but here.

I heard my mom and siblings come back home. I heard the laughter. I couldn't really hear what was being said, or what was happening. Time passed slowly in the crawl space. The darkness making each minute feel like an eternity.

A while later I heard his heavy footsteps on the stairs into the basement. Would he let me out now? Would he just make sure I was still there and then make me stay there all night? I prayed. I'm not sure why I bothered as I was certain God hated me more than I hated my stepfather. Maybe I was being punished because I didn't love him, and I was supposed to. The church said I was supposed to love my parents. But he wasn't my parent.

I heard him open the lock and the door swung open. "Get out." I scooted my butt across the dirt. I climbed out. The light in the basement hurt my eyes. I could barely open them after my time in the pitch black of the crawlspace. "When I tell you to eat, when I tell you to do something, you damn well better do it. I work hard to provide for this family, and you are nothing but a spoiled, ungrateful little bitch. I'll beat that out of you." I nodded in understanding.

Sadness was visible on my mom's face. Sadness and worry. She could not save me. He had no problem beating her as well or even anyone who happened to show up and try to intervene. While I had a strong imagination, I didn't ever manage to anticipate that things could continue to get worse. It seemed each time some new punishment was found and delighted in that I thought this was as bad as it would get unless or until he just managed to kill me. I also imagined that might happen quickly; a fit of rage and I'd just be gone.

Do What I Say

The rules in the house
Would never make sense

It was a 'do as I say
But not as I do' kind of world

Don't be a liar
But lie to me if it's what I want to hear

Don't be bad
But I'll be as bad as I please

Fits of rage
Taken out on a child

Spit in her face
Slap her until she falls down

When your anger is sparked
The fists will reign

She has taken more hits
Than a heavyweight boxer

Do what I say and love me despite what I do
But that's not how it will work for you.

The crawl space was a new form of punishment. He also knew that I feared things like centipedes. He knew that I wasn't fond of complete darkness. He'd found a new form of torture for me. It became fun for him, I think. There was dominance, a complete control that he could force on me. How powerful that must have made him feel.

The crawl space was not the end of it. We lived on a farm. A farm two miles outside of town, a quarter mile from our nearest neighbors, surrounded by fields. In the summer, those fields were high with corn or soybeans and for a young girl they seemed endless and huge. When the corn was high it towered over me. Who knew what could be in those fields? As children we were warned about little kids who had wandered into fields to never be found again, or to be found only when they were run over by a tractor or combine.

This created a new form of torture for me. One punishment didn't necessarily end when he found a new one, he just added new pieces to it. So, there was still the verbal abuse. I was called a names and belittled any time I made him angry through my own actions or just by simply being. New punishments were just a way to add terror and to keep me very aware that my life was in his hands.

The next piece after the crawl space was to make me go outside after dark, after he'd beaten me, he'd make me go out to a tree that sat closest to the field. From the house he would walk me out past the garage and then out past the flower garden to the tree that sat between the shed that housed all the tractors and combines and the chicken coop. I wasn't able to clearly see the house from where he'd put me, as the garage sat between that tree and the house. The wind would sometimes be blowing and the noises as it went through the corn fields used to scare me. I was too afraid to go someplace else, I wouldn't know if he came out of the house and if I wasn't where he had left me it would be worse for me. I'd sit up against the tree, trying to make myself as small as possible, nightgown tucked around me, so that if anything came out of the corn fields or from somewhere in the yard I'd not be noticed and sitting like that helped to keep me a little warmer on cool nights.

One moment he could be laughing and joking and the next his entire face and body posture would change, the yelling would begin, and a fist or open hand would come across your face, the belt would come off and the punishment for some known or unknown infraction would begin.

An interesting thing happens when you are this broken, your mind begins to find ways to survive. I had always loved it when my Avo would make up stories and tell them to me. As I got older, I began to read more books. I began to go inside my mind, into the stories I'd read, and, in my mind, I'd be in those places, doing the things the characters were doing. I could be terrified of what was happening to me, but I could be only partially there. Aware of what was happening to me, of the pain, of the body fluids, I heard the words and yet a part of me was in those books, living another life, a life where there was adventure, love, and laughter.

This may have saved some piece of me from completely breaking and being unable to come back. I wished for death, I hoped for a savior - not like Jesus, an actual savior to take me away and make me safe. I made up my own stories, I became brave, I saved myself in that world I created that was safe, where I was strong, where I couldn't be hurt.

As I got older new ways to harm me would come; I had never imagined it could get worse, but it did. Sometimes we believe we are experiencing suffering at its most extreme case. Frequently, we find out how very wrong our naive mind can be.

Splitting

Darkness descends as the little door closes
Even when my eyes adjust there is nothing I want to see

Dirt floor beneath me, boards above me
My small body hunched over

Bare feet in the dirt
I feel the little legs crawling over me

I hate the bugs
I want to scream

Screaming would not help at all
It would only feed his pleasure

My mind begins to shift
One part remains present the other goes away

Far off places I've read about it books
Heroines who save the day

I spent many hours becoming them
Adventuring in far off places

The mind of a child can shatter and break
Or go off the edge to a different place

A split between reality and fantasy
To help me survive this fate.

For some instances of abuse, I can't recall the infraction or slight that I did which offended him and created the abuse. There were so many instances and truth be told I could sigh or say hi with the wrong tone or volume. He'd wake up in a rage sometimes. The beatings, the anger and the punishments didn't only impact me. My mom would be woken up and dragged from bed, forced to call someone who he felt had slighted him or wronged him and wake them. He'd tell her what to tell them. Her voice would be shaking, he'd be screaming so they could hear him, but he'd expect her to repeat what he was telling her to tell them. The rage didn't need a rhyme or reason, it just was.

I don't know what caused this next situation, I imagine in his mind it was far greater an offense than it was in reality. What I do know is that instead of the normal routine he became so enraged while whipping me with his belt that he walked into the hallway, opened the closet, and pulled out the attic stick. The attic stick was called such because in the 3-bedroom ranch farmhouse there was an attic that had stairs which folded up and went up into the ceiling. To pull the stairs down there was a stick, roughly the size and shape of a police baton with a nail at one end that had been bent into the shape of a hook. You would take the stick, reach up and hook that bent nail into the hook on the staircase door, pulling it down to climb up to the attic. He pulled out this attic stick and walked back into the living room where I was. He began hitting me with it. He was spitting as he yelled at me. Spit streaming out of his mouth with every word. My arms went over my head to protect myself. The hits got harder. Every part of my body was being hit with this baton. My head, my arms, my neck, my back, my stomach, my chest, my legs, even my face. I'd drop to the floor and be yanked up. Finally, I was in a heap on the living room floor, my body screaming.

He dropped the attic stick and began kicking me with the boots he wore on the farm. Snub nosed cowboy boots. He kept kicking me, while telling me I was "A worthless piece of shit" "A good for nothing whore" "A bastard." The world faded; I could not see as clearly as I had. There was blood in my mouth, I could taste it, like metal. The sounds became muffled, the kicks I could feel and yet I felt as if I was floating. The world turned black.

I woke up in my bed. There were towels underneath me, I could feel them under my fingertips. The sun was shining, I could tell because the light was bright even though my eyes were closed. I knew that this had happened in the late afternoon. Was it the next day? I didn't know. I could hear sounds. I couldn't move my body though, my arms and legs felt heavy and the desire to move them didn't make them move. I couldn't seem to open my eyes. Everything hurt, my entire body felt like it would never again work. There was so much pain. My throat was burning. My limbs felt

I heard someone coming into the room. It was my mom. I could tell. I tried to open my mouth to talk but everything hurt. I couldn't seem to form words. She took a wet washcloth and wiped my face. The warm washcloth felt good. I was able to open one eye partially after that. Things were fuzzy looking. I couldn't focus correctly.

I laid in that bed for many days. I was fed broth and given water through a straw. I could barely open one eye and the other was swollen shut. I heard him come into the room many times and I simply pretended to be sleeping. He would start crying, saying how sorry he was. I didn't know if he was talking to me or to my mom. She didn't say anything to him either.

After a few days I was able to open one eye more, although the other stayed swollen shut for several more days. He would come in repeatedly crying. I could see that my body was black and blue. My lips felt swollen, and my legs and arms were still so heavy that I couldn't really move them without a great deal of pain. I also couldn't get myself to the bathroom, which was why there were towels under me.

When I was able to move again, I needed to be helped to the bathroom. I was peeing blood, which didn't really make sense then but as I got older, I realized I had been peeing blood from the damage internally done during beatings. I looked in the mirror and my face didn't look like my own. It was black, blue, purple, gray, there were so many colors and shades. Standing up made me dizzy and my legs shook.

I spent several weeks in that bed. The school was told I had gotten a very bad cold.

He apologized, so many times, crying while he did so, but I knew this was just in this moment. My young mind wanted to believe he was really sorry and yet I also knew nothing would change. Maybe I should have felt bad for him, the bible said we had to forgive people if we wanted to be forgiven. What a twisted hell the parts of the bible that people like to point out created in my young mind. Made to feel guilty for the pain caused to me by others even though

I wasn't in control of myself or them and then additionally, made to feel bad for my feelings of dislike, anger, hatred, because those weren't good feelings so having them somehow made me a bad person. Those twisted perceptions would affect me for many years.

I didn't go back to school until the bruises that could be seen when I was fully dressed were gone. No one questioned it. The teachers asked if I was feeling better. "Yes, thank you." I'd reply. I was feeling better. I could use the bathroom again without assistance. I could walk. I could see out of both eyes. I wasn't dizzy when I stood. Yes, I felt better...physically.

How else could I answer? There was no one to help me. There were teachers I loved but I knew they wouldn't do anything; even the police had done nothing. Nor did my stepfather seem to care. Our local police officer had tried to confront him once, and he told him to get off his property or he'd kill him as he had no business interfering in family matters. The police officer left. I had already seen how adults and the justice system could let you down. Some teachers I thought might have known, this was later confirmed, but they couldn't help or didn't know how to help, these thoughts were also later confirmed. A teacher told me that she was so sorry for what I had gone through, but that when she and a couple others had spoken to our principal, he had told them that they needed to mind their own business and not get involved or they could lose their jobs. It was the 1980's, people didn't get involved, they just talked about it in hushed tones.

Destroy

A grown man over six feet tall
Bulging muscles on his tanned arms

Those arms could have been used to hold and protect
But he chose to use them to destroy

They destroyed the innocence of a young child
They pummeled her small body

Whether by slaps, or fists, or belts, or objects
He'd beat her to his satisfaction

Destroying her innocence
Destroying her trust

Ruining her chances of believing in love
Destroying her mind with each blow

He beat her often
He tried to break her mind, body, and soul

This small child she was
Learned how to break away and protect a piece of her
sanity

She felt every blow and heard every word
She took them to heart

She didn't realize there was something stronger though
Something in her mind that kept her from being completely
broken

He tried to destroy her and came so close
Now his old body betrays him and is breaking down

While she has healed each trauma
Clearing away the harm rather than letting it destroy her
over time.

Once I was sent to my room for something I had done or said that he didn't like. No beating just sent to my room. My friend called the house to ask what I was wearing the next day to church. He came to my room and told me my friend was on the phone. I said, "But I thought I had to stay in my room the rest of the night?" He said to come answer the phone call.

I walked down the hallway to the kitchen, the only place there was a phone, and grabbed the receiver putting it to my ear "Hello?" All the while aware that he was standing just to the side of me, watching. "I'll wear a dress, not a skirt." I hurried to finish the phone call up. I was confused. I knew being sent to my room meant no phone calls, but I didn't know why he had allowed me to take this call.

I wrapped up the call quickly, it had lasted under two and a half minutes. I hung up the phone and as I turned and mumbled a "thank you" a fist hit me in the temple. My head hit the tile along the wall in our kitchen and I dropped to the floor. I didn't lose consciousness, "Stand up and get to your fucking room. I told you to go to your room. Why did you have your friend calling you? You always think you're fucking smarter than everyone don't you?" I mumbled "I'm sorry. I didn't know she would call."

"Get the fuck up and go to your goddamn room. You don't come out until tomorrow." I went on shaky legs and with a pounding head to my room, I sat on my bed waiting to hear him walk back to my room and open the door. Thankfully, that night that was all that happened to me.

I sat on the bed for a long time. No tears, but a headache had started. I thought about the events of the night. I made him mad just before dinner. He sent me to my room, no beating beforehand. Then let me take a phone call only to hit me after I hung up the phone, even though I had made the phone call quick. Even when I played by his rules I still got hit. It didn't make sense. Maybe he was crazy, and I was just in a home with a madman. *'It's not him, you're a stupid, spoiled little bitch, that's why this keeps happening. When are you going to learn your lesson? Why do you always think you are smarter than him? He's going to kill you one of these days because you are pathetic and don't deserve to live."*

That voice had started to keep me company. In the darkness of the crawl space, in the dark night with the sounds that I could hear but couldn't see what made them, in school, in my room, in the silence that voice kept reminding me of all the things he told me. That voice, I'd later find, would stay for a lifetime, even when I thought I had exorcized it, it would suddenly make an appearance and throw me off whatever I was hoping to accomplish."

Echoes

The words you once spoke to me
Echo in my mind
Sabotaging me at every turn

I don't want to believe those words
Because they came from you and you're no good
But they whisper insidiously somewhere deep inside

I hate the things they tell me
The questions they raise when I feel so good
Making me question everything I want and everything I
want to be

'You're never going to be good enough, you're just a fraud'
'No one can love a broken girl' 'all you are is a stupid
whore'
I hate these words, I try to push them down

They whisper in my head when I least expect
When things are going well
They set out to change my course

It's like you planted the seed
And though you are gone from my life
They continue to grow and take root

I'm left with the echoes of you
Still seeking to destroy all that is good in me
Trying to pull me back into the past

That's all that's left of you now
My life goes on without you

Reducing you to faint whispers and lonely echoes

In the fourth-grade things really began changing, I got a training bra. It was a sign of growing older. I thought that the entire thing was annoying. My mom took me to the store and made it into a big deal. The saleswoman took a measuring tape and measured around my chest right in the middle of the floor while making comments about training bras and little buds. I was mortified.

New bra. New school year. My second-grade teacher was now my fourth-grade teacher. She still didn't like me. She didn't realize that I needed to prove that I wasn't stupid, like he said, like that voice in my head kept reminding me that I was. I needed to be smart, it was more important than it should have been. In her defense, signs of trauma were not necessarily something most teachers at my school even knew about. The study of trauma was not something that was common and discussed like it is today.

Through all this I had a best friend, since school had started, she was my absolute best friend. She knew things weren't perfect. I told her on many occasions that I hated him. When I lived in the apartment in town, I had told her about him hitting me. She knew some things, but we were just kids and there was nothing for her to do but she understood me, and she loved me. Since we lived in such a small town there was only one class per grade, so we were always together. She made me laugh, she made me feel good, she loved me even if I was stupid, and all the things he and that voice told me. She saved me every single day of my life in that small town where most of the adults knew but didn't involve themselves. All I know is that when it comes to best friends, she has been by my side through it all for all these years and that makes me a very lucky person.

Fourth grade also brought about a change in my chores around the house. I was in charge of cleaning out the sow pens and the piglet pens with the power washer on the weekends and helping with feeding the baby piglets. This meant I spent far more time in the barn, with him, than I had before. There was not a choice in this. I hated the smell of the pigs, I hated that we raised them. I hated that the smell never fully left my nostrils. I did the work, and I did it well for fear that I'd be beaten if I didn't, even if at times the smells made me gag.

As I was finishing up the power washing one morning and putting things away, he was sitting on a 5-gallon bucket smoking a pall mall. "I heard your mother took you to the store to get a training bra." My back was to him. Why had my mom told him this? He knew our every move; I shouldn't have been surprised. I looked at him and nodded. "Your mom has nice tits. I hope you do too." *What? Why did he hope I did? Why was this conversation happening?* "Can I go up to the house and get cleaned up now? I'm supposed to go with mom to get groceries." He nodded and I left.

I took my shower, and I kept playing the conversation over and over in my mind. Why had he said that? I was a kid. He was an adult, my stepfather. That wasn't okay. No one had ever said something like that had happened to them. I had never heard of it. My friends had their real dads or no dad. I couldn't ask anyone.

I got dressed and went with my mom to the grocery store. Nothing else happened that day. I didn't mention it to her. The whole thing just made me uncomfortable. Not long after this incident, as my mom was making breakfast, he called me into his room to walk on his back. He had a bad back from being in the army and from farm work; he had once fallen from the top of a silo and landed on a haystack that had a pitchfork sticking out of it. It had gone through his thigh; he had told us. I shouldn't have but I often wished I could turn back time, so he had landed on it differently and died.

I went into the room and walked on his back. It was something he had made me do since I was young. I hated it. Sometimes he'd make me rub his back. Afterwards I'd wash my hands for long minutes because touching the back of the person who beat me senseless was abhorrent to me.

I finished walking on his back and he told me to rub his back. He started turning over. I stepped back. His hand went to my chest. From over my nightgown I was wearing, he touched my breasts "They are starting to grow. I like them" he said. I stood there motionless. I wasn't sure what to do. "You like that don't you?" he asked. I shook my head and whispered "No!" He laughed. "Someday you will." He reached down and pulled the hem of my Holly Hobbie pink nightgown up so that his hand could reach inside. He again touched my breasts. I was shaking. His hand went lower to my panties. He slid a finger between my legs, still outside my panties. "So nice," he said. I began shaking.

He took his hand away. "Don't say a word to your mother. I'll kill you if you do." I nodded my understanding. I believed him. He would kill me; he could kill me, and no one would do anything to save me or to stop him from doing it. Even if he did do it, nothing would happen to him, and I'd just be gone. I left the room and went to the bathroom, locking the door, turning on the water, scrubbing my hands over and over and then sat on the floor crying and shaking.

What had just happened? This was not okay. I didn't know what to do. There was no one I could go to or ask. I didn't want to die. He'd kill me and bury me on the farm. No one would even know I was gone, except my mom and my siblings. Would anyone miss me? Kay would. She would miss me. She would ask questions, but she couldn't do anything. I thought maybe I'd ask her about it, but then I realized he'd probably just kill her too and who would know. We were just kids. No one would ever find out; we'd just be dead. I stopped crying after a little while, my mom knocked on the door telling me to hurry up and I said I'd be out in a minute. I washed my hands again, I scrubbed them, they were bright red when I got done. I walked to the kitchen with my head down trying to avoid eye contact and ate my breakfast. Thankfully, my brothers were being annoying, so no one noticed me.

My Body

Before five years old, I knew I wasn't safe
My body bruised and beaten by huge fists
Slaps across the face and knocked to the ground

Open hands or closed fists, it didn't really matter
The results remained the same
Bruised and battered body struggling with the pain

Words spewed with venom
Cutting deeply from the inside
Mind shattering, trying to protect, but shattered
nonetheless

Lies and truths mixed up
Because lies needed to be told as truths
Convincing an abuser, in order to survive his assaults

Creating stories and hoping they would satisfy
They would reduce the number of strikes to my body
And stop the onslaught of hatred sticking in my brain

Biblical quotes used as weapons to get what was wanted
Confused by the use of scripture
To support the behaviors of grown men.

My body growing and changing created more unwanted
attention
Confused now by slick compliments from someone more
than twice my age
Combined with threats if those things were repeated

Learning again that compliance and pain go hand in hand
Compliance doesn't take away the pain, it changes the
pain
The bruises no longer visible as a colorful painting of
blues, greens, and purples

Instead as my body changes, his game does too
The cruelty warps and confuses and creates shame
Now I feel dirty and worthless in new ways, every day.

Sexual abuse. I didn't even know the term for what had happened. I didn't understand things like that because these were not normal conversations anyone had with children. I just knew I didn't like how my life was, but I'd have been happier with the previous abuse continuing rather than this. The back rubs or walking on his back were frequent and always had been. It had never been weird; gross but commonplace and not interpreted as anything out of the norm. He had a bad back and some people in the house were too heavy to walk on his back and others too light. I happened to be just the right weight...and this meant I was the one who went in the bedroom in the mornings to walk on his back while he laid in the bed in his white underwear or his long johns with a sheet over him.

After I had walked on his back or rubbed it the way he wanted he would roll over and tell me what I was supposed to do. Sometimes he would put his hand over mine to show me what he wanted and then I would be expected to continue. This was the training. This was when I learned to do what he wanted me to do. It was expected and I had no choice but to do it. I tried to refuse early on when the sexual abuse began and then instead of him being nice to me; I would end up getting slapped. Sometimes he'd find or make up some transgression I had committed and then he'd get out of bed and get his belt and whip me. I learned that I was to do what he wanted, exactly as he had shown me, and if I didn't do it, if I didn't act without argument or hesitation I would be hurt in other ways, often at other times as punishment for failing. It was a very twisted situation and one that created a lot of harm in my mind and took many years to work through.

As I'd do what he wanted his hand would wander up my nightgown, rubbing his hands over my body. Over the months he began to do more and more. I remember praying for it to go quickly so that I could leave. I'd literally pray "God, please let this be done fast. Make him hurry up." Afterwards I'd always run to the bathroom, I'd cry, I'd wash myself. I'd wish he would die.

I felt dirty, and gross, and I hated my body, if I didn't have this body this wouldn't be happening to me. I internalized everything as my fault. I had somehow caused this. It is so frightening how we see ourselves because of what others have perpetrated against us.

In the fifth grade we had a presentation done by our coach and our teacher. It was about sexual abuse. It explained things that I immediately recognized as what was happening to me. They passed around a pamphlet (there was only one) which we looked at. They talked about reporting those things because adults could help. I knew that was not true. Adults didn't help. No one would help and if I told anyone he would kill me, or he'd kill my siblings or my mom. He had told me as much and I believed him more than I believed in God, and heaven and hell! I also knew that many people in town were scared of him and steered clear. Adults were not going to help me.

I got the idea that if I could just show him the pamphlet, I could explain that what he was doing was wrong and he shouldn't keep doing it. I'd tried the argument before, and he had simply twisted the Bible to create a reason it was fine. As we were getting ready to go to lunch and then recess, I made my way to the table that had the pamphlet and grabbed it, intending to fold it up and take it home. My teacher caught me. She caught me with the pamphlet and loudly made a scene about it. She asked if I was trying to take it. I said I just wanted to look at it again. "What on earth is wrong with you Patty? Why would you want to look at that? Give it here and go to lunch." I handed it back to her. I turned and my best friend was there to walk with me. She asked why I had tried to steal it. I replied that I couldn't tell her. A couple of kids made jokes about why I would want to look at that stupid pamphlet again. None of them, not even a teacher who had just presented on the topic of sexual abuse, could imagine that I was being sexually abused. Our coach was in the doorway and witnessed this exchange but neither adult thought to ask if something was happening to me despite the fact that they had just finished presenting about sexual abuse.

That weekend while doing chores in the barn I tried to have a conversation with my stepfather. I realize as I write this that I have always believed in the power of words even before I realized that I did. I started by telling him that the teacher had given a talk about something called sexual abuse. He stopped what he was doing and turned around but didn't yell and his eyes hadn't changed. I had hope. I told him what it was, and I told him that what he was doing to me was exactly that and so it wasn't okay and he needed to stop doing it. He smiled just a little. I thought for a moment that I had made him realize it wasn't okay. Then he said "You're not my daughter and it would only be wrong if I was related to you, but since I'm not it's fine. I hope you didn't tell your teacher that I was doing something wrong to you. In the Bible men marry girls younger than you and have babies with them." What? No! That's not what they said, it could be strangers or people you knew, adults doing that to children. I tried to explain this part and he laughed. "Patty, I can do whatever I want with you. You're not my daughter, you are nothing but a bastard and even if you told them, do you know what would happen? You'd get in trouble, not me." I put my head down to try to think. I didn't believe him. He was a liar, a sexual abuser, and a mean person. "That's not true." I finally said. Looking at him with defiance, but I knew I'd pushed too far. I saw the change in his eyes. He walked across the distance between us in just a few strides and grabbed my hair "You stupid, little bitch, you're not good for anything but laying on your back like a fucking whore. Do you really think anyone would believe you? You don't even have a dad who wanted you. I ought to just kill you. Maybe I should kill your stupid whore of a mother and your brothers and your sister and then kill you too. Is that what you want? You would be the reason they all die! It would be your goddamn fault." He let go of my hair and grabbed my chin making me look up at him again but this time squeezing my chin between his big fingers "You shut your mouth and do what you are told, you will never be anything more than a stupid whore."

Tears were streaming from my eyes. He squeezed a little harder and bent his body so that I was looking up at him and his eyes and mine were looking right into each other's. Then he let go of me and told me to finish my chores. I finished them through tears. There was no point in trying to reason with him. He would do what he wanted, and the pamphlet was wrong, there was not a single adult who would save me or could stop him.

I was trapped, I didn't have any way out. Maybe when I turned eighteen, I could leave, but would he let me? Would

I live until then? A part of me wanted to die and yet a bigger part of me desperately wanted to live and be free of him.

Help Me

See me, help me
The mantra repeats in my head
As our teacher shows us the pamphlet

They talk about indicators
And it seems so obvious to me
That someone should see me, help me

Abuse in many forms
From fists and blows
That send my body into walls

Abuse in other forms
Rough hands
Touching parts of me that shouldn't be touched

See me, help me,
Save me from this hell
Why don't you see what creates my pain

Fear keeps me silent
Fear keeps me compliant
To demands that make me feel less than human

See me, help me
I want to be seen
I need my voice to be heard

The cry in my head
Never finds a way out
I sit here quiet and sad and scared

See me, help me
Why can't anyone see
The pain and harm being caused

See me, help me
Why does no one help
Save me from this man

As I got a little older, the sexual abuse changed. He wanted more things. Again, he would show me what he wanted or explain it and I would do what I was told to do. If I tried to refuse, he'd remind me of the pain he could cause, the harm he could cause to those I loved. I didn't understand why he would say that about my siblings, they were his children, and he didn't hit them like he did me, but I believed he was capable of everything he said he would do. I believed him and so I did what he wanted.

The sexual abuse continued to evolve; to become more than it had started as. He told me what he wanted and expected. My fear kept me in line. If I physically couldn't do what he wanted I knew punishment would be delivered. I wouldn't know exactly when, but it would happen. One day when I hadn't done exactly what he wanted he sent me to my room. Later he called the house and had me sent down to the barn. I didn't want to go down there. I also knew that I had no control of the situation, and I'd have to pay for my failure earlier in the day. As I walked into the barn, he grabbed me and punched me in my stomach. Again and again, he punched me. When he was done, he reminded me that I was worthless. I was on my knees. Tears streamed down my face. He left the barn and told me to get myself under control and get to the house.

I walked out of the barn a little later and slowly made my way to the house in the evening light. My stomach hurt and I thought I might throw up. I didn't think I could eat my dinner and said that I had a stomachache and was excused. I went to bed wondering if I could run away and survive. Even as I lay in bed fantasizing about how I could live on my own and escape this hell, I knew that it wouldn't work but I let it play out in my head anyway, a reprieve for my brain from what had occurred that day.

This was a coping mechanism. I created better places to be in my head and I went there whenever I needed to. It helped. It worked. I was checked out to some degree and it didn't allow my mind to consider the situation or go insane because there was nothing, I thought I could do to change what was happening.

Daddy

How do I tell you
What it is that I feel
When we both know
That my words will
Hurt you and in turn
Bring harm to me

You ask me what
Haunts my soul
What is it that supersedes all else
These things that awaken me
Throughout the night

These are the things
That eat at me each day
The mistakes and bad judgment
Calls I have made
Words misspoken and actions misrepresented

The flurry of things
That should have been
Overload my brain
Each being replaced by the next
A fight within myself about
What should be my next step

Can someone help to ease
What torments me each day
There is no cure for this torture
The fear and insecurity
Rule my every action

I pray for relief from this pain
Oh God help me!
I can't make it all go away
Lord, do I deserve this punishment
Can I offer it up to you?

Will you still love me
When you possess
The knowledge of my suffering?
The visions will haunt you
Even into your dreams

I warn you now
Before I go too far
Perhaps it's better to bear it alone
Because if I ever see a look of loathing
In your eyes it would be more
Than I can bear

Think long and heard
Before you ask me to proceed
The things you will hear
Will remain forever in the
Deepest recess of your mind,
Never leaving you

Imagine me young and tiny
Yet strong
Intelligent and pretty
With a light that burned inside
Allowing me to envision myself
Conquering all

There I am, you see me now
The long auburn hair and
Eyes so brown
My smile flashing, my skin unmarred
Do you see me
Hold that image, for it will soon be gone

Follow me now
to the beginning of my pain
When church bells rang
As if announcing the change
Noone knew then but they do now
The monster that would reside in my home

What should have been joy
Lasted none too long
For soon there would be shouts
And shattering blows
Noone could stop the monster
Who raged behind closed doors

The blows to my tiny frame
Left scars and bruises
Too many to name
My lithe little body, no longer unmarred
It now bore witness
To the pain received

I'd fall into a heap
Upon the floor
Trying to escape the reach of his blows
I was no match,
He'd grab me and throw me
And then beat me some more

Day after day, year after year
I endured and I suffered
Because nobody cared
About one little girl
Who mattered not a bit
In this great big world

As I grew older, I grew wiser
I joined every sport and club
I went home with hope that
I could feign exhaustion
And be allowed to hide in
The solace of my room

Soon though that solitude
Was invaded by hands
Hard and calloused
Touching my skin
'Oh god, what now, when would this end'
Close my eyes, stop feeling

Words that made me ill
Whispered in my ear
Telling me I'm beautiful,
asking if I liked to be touched there
No, No, please, please stop!
"Shut up you little bitch!"

I'd close my eyes.
I couldn't fight I had to endure it
A word from me and my siblings die, then my mom
And then me
My silence was ensured

I endured his hands
Crying each time
My body would tremble,
My stomach always in knots
He liked what he saw and did what he did
His perversion enjoyed only by him

Soon, however, it wasn't enough
Now I needed to participate
He made me touch him,
While he guided my hands
Do you like this, he would ask
There was no escape

Soon though the game
Needed to change.
Not just my hands but now my mouth
I gagged, I choked, but he didn't care
One threat and I did what I was told
He liked the power

A threat here and there
Made me a good student
Who wants to see their
Baby brother murdered
I did what he said and didn't fight
Then cried myself to sleep at night

But, wait there is more
To this perverse tale
Why shouldn't he have me
Possess my body with his own
I fought, I scratched,
He seemed to like that even better

My body was taken,
All that I had was no longer mine
My stomach cramping
I scrubbed
I vomited
But nothing could make me clean

Can you now begin to see
The pain that was inflicted on me
I had no choice,
no path to take
Only to endure it
There was no chance of escape

There I was completely lost
Body shaking, sore and bruised
I knew I was worthless now
There was nothing left to lose
I was now just
Daddys little whore

As junior high was wrapping up, I had come to many realizations. He could not force me anymore. I mean, he physically could force me, but he had always made the sexual abuse very twisted. I knew I'd get beaten, I knew he could physically force me, I knew if I didn't do what he wanted there would be a punishment, but it didn't happen in that moment, or at least only rarely. It was done so that he could say that I had done those things to him willingly, that would be his argument. He had not forced me; I had done it on my own, even if he told me what he wanted I had chosen it. That is manipulation and grooming, but how would I know that? Sexual abuse was rarely talked about. I hadn't heard another word about it since fifth grade.

I felt shame, I felt self-hatred. I believed I was not a good person. He had taken me from being a little girl who was so secure in her family and love that she was confident and full of joy and laughter to a girl who faked what the world expected. I felt like a fraud. I was conflicted about God. How could a God exist if this were allowed to happen. I had read the book of Job at church because it was used as an example of having strong faith in spite of terrible tragedy and adversity. I read it and I was angry! God and Satan sat around and made a bet? A bet! And screwed someone's life up for a bet to prove someone's love? That was gross and disturbing to me. I was ashamed that I was mad at God, I had been taught that wasn't okay. I was a mess. I felt so conflicted about so many things.

There are hundreds (or more) other stories or instances in which I was beaten, I was verbally abused, I was sexually abused, but you have the general idea. There were not more than one or two weeks that there was ever a reprieve. I went to camps as often as I could. I involved myself in church youth groups, basketball, softball, track and field, band, math club, the spelling bee team, and 4-H. If it got me out of the house for a few additional hours I was willing to learn and be a part of it because it was something that could save me and help me avoid interactions and time with or around my stepfather. Sometimes he'd be asleep by the time I got home. Those were the best days. Other times he waited, awake, and would come into my room after I had fallen asleep to wake me up for whatever he wanted. The more groups and activities I could be part of meant I got to stay away from him for more hours. By being away from the house and him more, I was able to avoid some amount of abuse for longer periods of time. Maybe a few days, sometimes even longer. A week of no abuse was a blessing. It didn't happen frequently but when it did, it felt like I had won the lottery!

Every year I went to camp. As soon as I was old enough to go to camp I started going, I honestly jumped at the chance. I went every year, a week of church camp, a week of 4-H camp, if I could do both it would be even better! If I did both I had to pay for the second one, but 4-H allowed me to have money in the bank. I only made it a couple days at camp the summer after seventh grade, before getting sick. I mean, really sick. I couldn't hold anything down. I spent most of the week in the nurse's station throwing up and sleeping. I got home and immediately went to the doctor. I had mono. My stepfather and mom were there when the nurse said that I had mono which was called the kissing disease. I wanted to die because I saw the look that crossed my stepfather's face. As sick as I was, it did not keep him from interrogating me as soon as we got home from the doctor. Who had I been kissing? Why had I been kissing a boy? Had I had sex with him? I was nothing but a worthless whore. He was angry, telling my mom that I was worthless and that she had given birth to a child who would be nothing more than a whore. I told him over and over that I was not kissing anyone. I had gotten sick within days of getting there but I was lying. I had kissed a boy named Paul or rather, he had kissed me. The whole thing only lasted a second. We went to the lake on the second or third day and got a rowboat. We had rowed out toward the back of the lake. He talked about school and 4-H, and all the sports that he did. I talked about the same. When it was time to come back, he rowed us back to the dock, we got out and started walking towards the cabins, he stopped me and kissed me quickly, just a little peck on the side of my mouth. I would not tell my stepfather about this and no one else knew. So, I lied. I lied and I lied, and my mom finally got him to understand that they just call it the kissing disease because kids share drinks and food and spread it among themselves quickly. He finally left it alone.

It took weeks before I shook the effects of mono. Thankfully, the vomiting stopped after the first two weeks. He would press the issue again, trying to trip me up or get me to admit to kissing someone, but I held firm to the lie I had told.

I Say

I say what you want to hear
It's the only way to survive

I do what you want me to do
You don't care that I'm dying inside

I mimic the actions of my peers
In hopes that they don't see the charade

Or the lost young girl who lives inside
But is dead behind her smiling face

I want to seem normal
I really want to be

But there is something different
And that something is me

It's my fault, it's my doing
Something bad is inside me

I didn't mean to be bad
I don't want to be anymore

But here I go lying again
More lies each time that I need to survive

And I know that makes me terrible
But I say what I need to say to get by

I can fake the part of the happy girl
But I know it will never be me

Even if I escape this hell
I'm not worthy of the love I long for

I say what they want to hear
It doesn't matter who anymore

I'm happy
I say to the world

But deep down I know
That what he says is true

I'm nothing
I'm useless

I'm never going to be loved
I'm worth nothing to anyone

I'm stupid
I'm worthless

I know it to be true
I try to deny it but worthless is all I feel anymore

I want a good life
I want to be happy

But here we go again
I say what I need to say to survive.

A year later, I went to summer camp again. One of the first days there I told a girl who was assigned to the same cabin as me that a boy in line for lunch was cute.. She happened to be in the same 4-H group as him. She introduced me to him. He had a quick smile. He was a little older than me, he seemed so mature and sure of himself. We spent an entire week at camp together during the day and by the end of the week, I was sure I was in love. He lived in a different county than I did, and this was when people paid for long distance telephone calls by the minute. Every minute was charged, and I didn't realize how quickly that would add up. He called me and I called him. We even had taken a couple of polaroids together. I kept one and he kept the other.

Our phone calls created a problem. The phone bill was high and to try to hide it my mom made me pay for it out of my bank account. I gladly did so. She told me I had to stop calling, but even the threat of my stepfather being mad did not change that I wanted to talk to this guy so badly, partly because he made me feel like I was normal. I kept calling but tried to limit it so that it wouldn't be noticed on the phone bill.

My stepfather came into my room one day. He was asking me about something he needed me to help him write. As I got up to go to the den to help him, he noticed the polaroid. He picked it up. "What the fuck is this?"
'SHIT' I thought before answering "A boy from camp." I had been looking at it when he came into the room and had hastily thrown it on my nightstand when he walked into my room. I hadn't expected him to walk all the way over to my bed in the middle of the day.

He continued to hold the photo, grabbed my arm, and hauled me to the kitchen where my mom was making dinner.

"Maria, did you see this picture?" My mom answered that she had. "It's a cute picture."

No. No it was not. Not for my stepfather. This was not going to turn out okay.

"Look at her - she looks like a whore just wanting to get fucked" then turning to me "That's all you are, isn't it? Just a dirty, worthless fucking whore."

I said nothing. I was stone cold and angry. My heart rate had increased but not just out of fear. This was anger. I had so much anger. I was happier in that picture than I had ever been. Then he lit the picture on fire and lit one of his pall malls while holding it to watch it burn. I yelled "NO!" I reached for the picture to take it from his hand. He backhanded me. "You fucking whore. You just lay down for anyone, don't you? DON'T YOU?"

I was sent to my room. I heard him yelling, ranting, and raving. I cried for the loss of the picture. I cried because I hated him. I cried because I wanted to be somewhere, anywhere but in this house with him. I wouldn't do this anymore. I couldn't do this anymore. I would not let him do this to me anymore. The guy from camp knew that my stepdad was a terrible person. I hadn't told him everything, but I had told him enough that he knew I was in danger.

I continued talking to this boy. We tried to talk every day or every other day. I knew I had to hide it from my stepfather. I told him to hang up if my stepfather answered the phone. My mom knew we were talking because when she answered the phone, he'd ask for me and as long as my stepfather wasn't around, she'd let me talk to him. She didn't see the problem and until that phone bill came again, she didn't realize I had continued to call him too. While the charges didn't amount to much, because he would call me back, so I didn't get in trouble, they were still noticeable. I was in love and had fully lost my mind. I knew the consequences. I knew the beatings or other things would occur, but I was at a breaking point.

One day when my stepfather was out of town, for a visit to the VA Hospital and to get some supplies at the Big R store , I was doing my chores in the barn. That morning before he had left, he told me that I could talk to this boy but that meant he expected things in return, things that I needed to initiate without being told to do them. I didn't answer him in agreement or otherwise. I simply kept my head down and that seemed to satisfy him that I was thinking about it. After he left and had been gone for long enough that I knew he would not be turning around because he had forgotten something I called this boy. I told him what my stepfather had said. He asked if he had touched me before and I said that he had. He told me to tell someone, that I had to tell my mom. I was so broken, and I was fed up. I was angry. I hated my life. I hated my stepfather. I wanted out of this hell. I wanted to be normal. I wanted to have a boyfriend, to be like the other girls I knew. I wanted to be happy!

My sister walked into the barn "Mom said you better get off the phone."
I looked at her and I made a decision that changed everything! "Wait" I said to my sister as she was walking out the door of the barn. I got off the phone and decided I was telling my mom about the abuse. I opened the small cabinet that had pens and such in it. My sister had only

finished Kindergarten, so she couldn't read. I pulled out a pencil but there was no paper. I pulled an empty light bulb wrapper out of the trash can. I tore a piece of the paper off and wrote a note to my mom "He's been touching me for years." I handed it to my sister, telling her to give it to our mom. I dropped into a squatting position as she took the note and ran back up the drive to the house. After a short time, I thought 'Oh my god, stop her, what have you done? You can't tell anyone!' I ran to the barn door just in time to see my sister walk into the house.

It was done. My heart raced. I felt sick. What had I done?

The Telling

Hushed noises, dark rooms,
Silence demanded

Keep the secrets and stay alive
Reveal them and you might die

Secrets, secrets that no one knows
Just him and I

I don't want this anymore, I never wanted it
I've had enough, I can't live with this anymore

What can I do
Better to die at his hand

Than go on this way
Secrets locked in my soul

I write the note
I send it over

What the hell have I done
I don't want to die

I can't live this way though
What else is there to do

Take a chance
Send the word

Tell the secret
Let it go

Save me or end me
It will be one of the two

I just know
I can't live without telling anymore

The telephone to the barn rang. I picked it up but didn't say a word. The voice of my mother on the other end, was calm, slow, and one I wasn't prepared for, "Patty, come to the house." I walked slowly to the house. What would she say? What would she do? What could she do? He was stronger than all of us. I walked up to the house. I had been cleaning the barn, so she told me to go shower quickly and then come back to her. Tears were in her eyes. I wondered as I walked to the shower if her tears were the helpless tears I'd seen so many times before when he had beaten one of us and there was hurt and fear but not even my mom knew how to get out and stay gone.

I showered and changed, and she asked me to sit down. She asked two questions: "Is this true?" I nodded yes. "How long has it been going on?" I told her. Tears rolled down her cheeks. She made some phone calls, I don't remember who the calls were to, or what was said, my heart was pounding so hard, my thoughts were racing. We went to our neighbor's house. I loved our neighbors deeply, they were so kind, genuinely good people. My mom and the neighbor sat in the other room while my sister, brothers, and I watched T.V. I heard them talking. I could make out bits and pieces. "You have to tell him it can't happen again. The same thing happened to me when I was little, but these are not things people talk about. Where would you go? How will you take care of the kids without him?"

I've said before, the 80's were a different time, central Illinois was an entirely different place with lots of Bibles on tables and nightstands, Sunday services, and good Christian farm families. I don't blame anyone who said things that had been ingrained in them. Those same people have shown me such kindness over the years that I could never think less of them for it. It was a different time, a different way of living, and many of those people just simply didn't know a better or different way.

My mom wasn't having it. She contacted the Illinois State Police. It took a while, but they met us and we went to the farm with the officer. We were told to go to our rooms and pack a few things. I went to my room. I wanted to take things that mattered, not just clothes, but that wasn't what we had been told. I helped my sister pack a few things too.

I walked back to the kitchen to find that my stepfather had returned to the house while we were in the bedrooms packing things. He was standing in the kitchen along with the state police officer and my mom. She was scared. I was scared. He was being very soft spoken, the way he did when others were watching, (I never understood when people didn't see through that charade) and if we were left there and the officer wasn't there, we would pay dearly for embarrassing him, for causing him trouble. The police officer wasn't nearly as big as my stepfather, but he did have a gun, maybe this day was not the day that I'd die.

My stepfather looked at me. I saw a rage stronger than I had ever seen before. Maybe he was going to kill me. The officer got his attention and told him that my mother could choose to contact him if she wanted. The officer told us to go ahead and walk outside and for my stepfather to stay in the house. My sister and brothers had walked towards my mom, so everyone had gone out the backdoor except for me. I had stopped in my tracks on the other side of the table when I came into the room and hadn't moved around the table closer to my mom and the officer while they had talked, so as I began walking towards the door, even the police officer had walked out ahead of me. As I came around the table to go out the door my stepfather leaned forward and whispered, "I'll kill you for this." I ran past him, shaking from head to toe.

That evening we drove to the town my aunt and uncle lived in, almost four hours away. My mom told me on the ride up that she had called my aunt and told her we were coming and why. I was scared, what would my aunt and uncle think of me? Mom asked several times on the car ride why I hadn't told her, and she cried a lot and apologized more times than I could count. In the darkness I could hear her, and knew she was crying but I was glad that I could just look out the passenger window as the lights from the cars sometimes illuminated our faces, and just shut out the world. I didn't know what I felt. I was still scared. I was still confused about so many things. I was relieved that she had left. I feared what would happen next.

When we arrived at my aunt and uncles, my aunt ran out and grabbed me with both hands by the face, kissing me, speaking loudly in Portuguese, asking why I hadn't told anyone. They all knew why. Everyone was scared of him. My aunts, my mom, my uncles. They all knew the monster he was, and no one had dared to make him mad. They knew why I hadn't told anyone, but they asked anyway. It was surreal. I was not in his house anymore. I wasn't there anymore but I knew that didn't mean he wouldn't show up in the middle of a night sometime and finish this once and for all. I went to bed that night safer than I had been in years, but not feeling safe or secure. Safety and security would not be a feeling I had for many years. I'd often wake up from nightmares, sweating, crying, shaking, and certain he was in the house and would kill me at any moment. I was free of him physically and spatially, but psychologically I was still fully in his grasp.

Freedom Comes

A chance was taken
Live or die - it didn't matter

It had to be one or the other
I couldn't take the lies and the pain anymore

I told the truth
And it set me free

Long car ride in the night
That took me to freedom from this pain

I was happy but so uncertain
I prayed to god that I'd be okay

Freedom from him should fix everything
Right the wrongs that had been done

So young and unknowing that the damage was done
I'd struggle for years to come

But freedom came from the telling of my truth
From the single note scrawled on a piece of garbage

Freedom from those haunted days and nights
From the nightmare my life had been

Now I could just be, live the life of a girl my age
Be wild and free and who I was meant to be

I was given a chance and in that change
Freedom had come.

I didn't know freedom held a price
It was not something easy or nice.

Days and nights of struggle
A deep sadness that held me down

It strangled and terrified me
But I tried to smile and pretend everything was fine

Freedom came
But it didn't fix the wrongs and it didn't take away my
mental pain

Freedom simply changed the landscape
My mind was still a prisoner

I struggled to come to grips with everything
To merge what had happened and what could be

No one was able to explain what was wrong
Why couldn't I just be happy now?

Freedom has a fee
The echoes of his voice wouldn't let me be

Gasping for air as I woke
A cold sweat with clothes drenched

Tear stained face in the darkness
As I gained my bearings

Heart racing, was he in the house
Trying to think logically and remember I was safe

No monster hiding, lurking in the shadows
To carry out a promise whispered

Freedom had come
But mentally I was still living in fear

Here I was, living in my aunt's home. I had an older cousin to whom I had always looked up. I was named after her. The reason I was named the same as my cousin was because my mom and her sisters all decided to name one of their daughters Patricia. I was "little Patty" in the family. The middle one was the one I looked up to and was closest to. She was also the daughter of my aunt whose house I was living in. My older cousin graduated the year before we moved. She was working and seemed so grown up compared to me. It's interesting the way we idolize people, and sometimes those lofty beliefs fall terribly short of what we had made them out to be in our minds.

She got me a day or two after we had made it to town. She told my mom we were going to see a movie and grab some dinner. My mom gave me money. As soon as we got out of the driveway my cousin said to hand her the money. I was annoyed, "I'm old enough to take care of my own money." She yelled at me to give her the money. I handed it over. I didn't know what her problem was, but I wasn't going to argue, besides, she was my favorite cousin.

She proceeded to pick up a couple of her friends and we went to her boyfriend's house. She handed him money and they talked a bit. I was being introduced to people and I really didn't know who was who but someone handed my cousin's boyfriend a bag and then left. He was back a while later and there were bottles of alcohol. I asked if I could play the Nintendo that he had. I sat down on the floor playing. My cousin's boyfriend came and grabbed the other controller. People were smoking cigarettes. The trailer was getting smoky. Her boyfriend and I continued playing Nintendo. I liked my cousin's boyfriend; he was nice to me and hung out with me while everyone else was drinking and smoking.

After my cousin had smoked a few cigarettes, drank a bit, and smoked what was in the bag with her friends she told me to come over to them. Her boyfriend protested "Come on, leave her alone. She's just a kid." I got up and walked over. She handed a bottle to me and told me to drink it. I smelled it and declined. She told me to drink it. I told her I didn't want to. She stood up and pushed me back in a chair, straddled me and told me to drink "I'm not having your little goody two shoes ass going home and telling your mom and mine that I was doing bad shit. If you say anything you'll be in just as much trouble as me. You're gonna drink this." Her boyfriend jumped up and protested, "C'mon, she's just a kid. Leave her alone." She told him to shut up, proceeded to push my head back and hold my jaw while she poured whatever it was into my mouth, she then shut my jaw and held it. "Swallow it" I did. We repeated this a few more times. Her boyfriend was quiet after that and just gave me a sad look and said he was sorry very quietly.

The rest of the night I was dizzy, I felt like I was going to throw up, and I felt kind of mad. My cousin took me home later. The next day when my mom asked about my night, I said we had fun, and the movie was great. Thankfully, she didn't ask what movie.

After that I just took a drink when we were together, slowly I began drinking more. It started numbing my feelings. I also started smoking weed with her. I didn't feel so scared all the time when I was drinking. I could laugh and really mean it, not just fake it to fit in or hide things. Sometimes they did other things but when I asked about it, she told me to mind my own business and not touch anything else. I listened. She wasn't the same person I had always looked up to. She wasn't as nice as she used to be.

She never asked me about my stepdad or the things that had happened to me. She was probably the one person I'd have been able to talk to, but she had become someone I didn't recognize and after a while, I also was someone I didn't recognize.

Now, you'd think that being out of my stepfather's house and someplace safe would make me feel safe and everything would be great, right? I certainly thought that should be the case. I didn't understand when that wasn't the case. I didn't understand why I felt like I didn't fit in. I didn't know why people who were nice to me in class invited me to their table at lunch then sat me down with their friends and proceeded to make fun of me. I started staying to myself. I was a mess. I was lonely. I wanted to make friends. I missed my friends. I spent many evenings high, drunk, or both.

I hated everything. Within months I tried to kill myself. Someone at my school found me and although I ended up fine, it freaked him out and he talked to a teacher we both had. That teacher pulled me aside as we were beginning a new book in class that talked about a girl who attempted suicide. She told me that this boy had told her what had happened, how he had found me, and how it had scared him. She suggested that I go talk to the school counselor.

I talked to the school counselor. In so many ways I have regretted that decision for years. I have wondered many times over the years how things might have been different if I had not confided in her. I told her why I had done what I'd done. I told her that after leaving my abusive stepfather's home, I thought everything would be okay but instead I was lonely, I was afraid of everything, I didn't want to deal with the world, I hated myself and I finally just decided that it wasn't worth trying anymore. He had been right, I was worthless. I told her enough about the abuse to paint a clear understanding of what had been going on and led to the suicide attempt.

She reported this to DCFS. She was a mandated reporter, so I understand that, although at the time, I did not know anything about that or what confiding in her would mean in regard to her disclosing it to others. I ended up spending many hours being interviewed by two DCFS workers in an office at the high school, one was a caseworker, and one was that caseworker's boss. Multiple interviews occurred. All these happened during school hours. My mom had to come in. I didn't want my mom to know all the details. My mom had asked enough questions to understand what had happened, but not enough to require me to give all the details. They told me they had to share all the information with her. I hated that. I hated having to talk about it all repeatedly.

After that I felt like everyone was judging me. I was sure I was more trouble than I was worth. All I did was cause problems. Mom would have been happier if I hadn't been in the picture and maybe he wouldn't have done all the mean things to her if I hadn't been around. I was the problem. I certainly didn't feel better yet. If anything, I just kept feeling worse and worse.

Not long after having talked to the school counselor and the people from DCFS, I was walking from the cafeteria down the hall to a class. A girl was standing by her locker with several of her friends around her. One of her friends was the school counselor's son. She yelled my name. I turned to look at her, I had no idea who she was and as I was trying to think if I remembered her face from my classes she said "I hear you like fucking your daddy. You're a daddy fucker!" She threw back her head laughing. Her friends also started laughing. I felt my face go red, I felt my heart start racing, I felt the tears start burning in my eyes. I gripped my books against my chest as if they were some kind of protection, turned and started down the hallway as "Daddy fucker" was chanted and rang in my ears. I began to run. I ran right out of the school. I ran home. I sat alone, thankfully no one was home. I cried so much that afternoon. I hated everything. I didn't want to be here anymore. I didn't want to go back to that school. I couldn't. I told my mom. She wanted to go talk to the school. I refused. I missed the next couple days of school and didn't go back until the following week and even then, didn't want to.

I felt so much shame as I walked into the school. Children with a history of abuse and/or neglect frequently hear that it wasn't their fault, but the truth is people sure do make them feel like it is. Some people still made comments. I would have someone slide up next to me in the hall and say something like "What's up daddy fucker?" and then laugh and walk away, their friends laughing and finding it hilarious.

There were a few people who I befriended. Who either had no interest in what the sophomore girl and her friends had to say about me or were simply better human beings. I appreciated them. They are the reason I didn't make another attempt at my life. I remember someone saying, "I'm sorry that happened to you." I wasn't sure if they meant the abuse or the thing the girl and her friends were saying, but the kindness of that person felt like a lifeline I could hold on to.

The trauma hadn't stopped, it had only changed. I didn't know who I could trust or who was genuine and who wasn't. I wanted to just be normal, but no matter what I did, I just didn't feel normal. I also couldn't define normal. In my head it was that I wouldn't feel like I did and instead would feel happy again. I learned to protect myself in new ways and continued to use some of the old ways of coping. None of these really served me in healing or becoming who I wanted to be; but they did help protect me from who could hurt me, which at that time was pretty much anyone. It hurt, of course, but I just learned to show up ready to fight or act ice cold. It served me in high school, it helped create an image of me for others and most people stopped messing with me to my face, they were scared of me, or thought I was a bitch. In either case, I wasn't liked by the popular kids, but they were cruel and that was fine with me. People still talked. I'd hear things that were said but after a while they got bored and moved on to actively tormenting others. I was thankful for that and felt guilty that someone else was now the object of their torment.

The problem with these characters we create to protect ourselves is that we aren't being authentic, and it takes a lot to keep them up, we get more comfortable being in character, but we also continue to hurt on the inside, isolating ourselves and being at conflict in our hearts.

For Your Amusement

Things weren't great
I was trying to navigate this new life
I still wasn't well but I didn't understand why
I had so much pain that tore me apart.

Bad choices were made I took too many pills
I didn't die though but now people knew something was
wrong
Some were concerned, most probably were
I could no longer keep the secrets inside

I needed to find my way out of everything that had been
done to me
I spoke of my abuse, what else could I do
With this burden that was weighing me down
She was trusted, she was nice, she seemed caring and
supportive

I walked down the halls struggling to find peace
I had no friends here and missed my friends from home
I heard my name I turned around in the crowded hall
You looked at me and called out my shame for everyone
around to hear.

You called me names, while others began to laugh
I could hear it, I felt like the world fell out from under me
You laughed and you laughed as I turned around and ran
You broke me more than I had been, but you didn't care; it
was for your amusement

The chant rang in my ears and the hallway seemed so long
I ran for the side doors to get away from it all
My heart was racing as I headed towards home
Tears streaming down my face I hated my life, and I hated myself

My story had been told; my confidence betrayed
I was already broken and hurting but this changed me again
I knew I had to own my story and get a harder shell
Now I was angry and ready to fight

For your amusement you hurt someone who was so fragile
You thought you were cool and funny
But you never considered the harm to another
You never realized what it would cost me, it was done for your amusement

The wheels of justice turn slowly. Sometimes they come to a skidding halt. Sometimes they leave you in another wreck; leaving you wondering if the original crime caused you the most pain or if it was the justice system that created more damage. The way the justice system allowed you to be victimized on the stand, or the failure of the justice system in sentencing. All these things left me with additional harm. I questioned why it was worth talking to the authorities. I understood why people didn't report things to the police.

During my junior year we finally went to court. My freshman year, I had started out joining teams and clubs at school, but I couldn't keep it together and the stress, the frustration, the anger, the hurt all kept colliding. I spent time a lot of my time drinking, smoking pot, and pretending to be a much tougher person than I ever have been. Sophomore year was not too different. At 5'4" and not even 100 pounds, I was not an intimidating figure, so I figured out other ways to keep people away. I became aggressive. I was loud, I was in your face, I smoked cigarettes, I cursed. People were either going to completely leave me alone or be a bit scared of what kind of crazy was behind all that behavior.

By the time we went to court I had been dating this guy Bob for a while. He had a cocky smirk, quick-wit, and didn't seem at all bothered by my attitude or behavior. He was a skater boy (cue the nineties song). Toward the end of my freshman year, he asked me out. We started dating and kept dating. He recognized my damage and accepted it, and I accepted the same about him. We were kindred spirits. Two messed up kids, who didn't know how to fix themselves but were willing to try to help someone else be fixed. Trauma bonding. That's what we did and how we moved. We didn't have any business dating anyone, we didn't know how to help ourselves with the things we had dealt with, but here we were.

My junior year I decided to get myself together. I had always been smart, I did well on tests even if I never read the assigned pages. I could write an essay in the hour before a class and still get an A. I decided I really did want more out of life. I began taking things seriously. I wouldn't be the loser, or the screw up that I was starting to be labeled - that had been driven home by an assistant principal; I wanted to be something. I wanted my life and my time to mean something.

By the time we went to court about the abuse, Bob and I were a serious item. He wanted to go to court with me, to be the support I needed. Our school told him if he left for the time on my subpoena, he would be kicked out of school since he had not been summoned to court; he came with me anyway! Court was terrible. The lawyer for my stepfather tried to twist things and bring Bob into the entire situation asking if we were having sex, accusing me of being boy crazy and making everything up, demanding that I name instance after instance of abuse and when I would he would simply say "another." It was cruel and it was terrible. I was drained and angry and retraumatized repeating my story in a courtroom occupied by attorney's, a judge, DCFS caseworkers, and of course, my stepfather. I was still hopeful that he'd go to prison - surely if justice prevailed, I'd be better.

At the end of the week the judge looked at me, as he passed down his sentence. He told me that he believed that what I said had happened to me was true, he believed every single instance I had given had occurred and more. He said that he was sorry for what had happened to me, but I was one hundred fifty miles away from my stepfather and he couldn't hurt me anymore and of course, we wouldn't want him to lose his farm. He then proceeded to sentence him to some nights in jail and probation. I was stunned. He believed me…but the farm was more important than the harm that had been done to me, to my family. The judge believed me and yet my stepfather's farm was more important than the years of terror and abuse and torture. He believed me but from one hundred fifty miles away my stepfather couldn't hurt me anymore. He still hurts me every day, I thought! I woke up in a cold sweat. I woke up shaking. I dreamt of him. I was afraid of the dark. I was afraid to be alone. This was not justice! I left feeling like I had been kicked in the gut. I can't even fully describe it, but I can still feel it. The knot in my stomach, the emptiness, wondering why they even called it a justice system. I felt the dark cloud forming around me. Nothing was ever going to be put right. He should be in prison for all that he had done to me, to my mom, to my siblings. He was an animal, capable of terrible violence but he would remain free. It hadn't mattered!

This took me down another path of complete destruction. Who cared about school? Who cared about anything? I was worthless; even the justice system didn't place my body or what had been done to it as more important than farmland. Why had I bothered to believe that they would do something? Every time I was told by adults that they would prosecute him and make him pay for what he'd done, it had all been a lie. I had put my story and my truth out there, I had been vulnerable and scared but had done it anyway. All the hurt they had caused me to go through to sit and repeat story after story about the abuse in front of strangers. For what? A couple of nights in jail and some probation and ten years on the sex offender registry. This was not justice. This was just another layer of trauma.

I spiraled. I dropped out of high school. Despite some teachers, my mom, a wonderful dean all trying to convince me that I'd regret this decision later. I dropped out because I was too hurt, too harmed, too lost to continue pursuing something that seemed so pointless to me.

My mom finally had enough of the fighting, skipping school followed by dropping out, the drunk nights of stumbling in, the disappearances that sometimes-lasted weeks. We got into a fight, and she slapped me. I ran away. I don't know how long I was gone, a couple weeks, but when I came back a new approach was taken. We talked about me going to the community college to get my GED, about getting me a car, about getting to a better place mentally. I was somewhat on board; I didn't trust that it could happen. I was not getting better. I didn't want to be a loser my whole life, but I wasn't sure I wanted to continue this life at all. It was all pretty messed up in my head. Death seemed a good option, but I was also aware that life can't get better if you aren't here. To put it simply, I was hurt so deeply, and I had no idea how to get better. It seemed that the counselors and everyone around me were also at a loss for how to make me able to move forward. Shame and telling me what I was doing wrong were the tactics taken and for a girl already so deeply harmed and lost, that just didn't land well. I already lived with shame. Society was set up in a way that even as a child, shame was a built-in part of life. Shame and I knew one another very well.

Mom picked me up one morning with the plan that we were going to go to the community college to get the ball rolling for me to get my GED, then we were going to go look at a car. She told me she had to stop at the bank. She came out a few minutes later and my cousin was with her. They both opened opposite doors and sandwiched me between them. I was taken to a drug rehab center where I was admitted and told I was an addict. This was mostly because I had a terrible attitude and admitted to how much drinking and pot smoking, I had done over the years; my drug test was negative, but I did tell them about how much partying I had done. The rehab center people knew I had a problem, but they didn't understand my problem was unprocessed trauma not addiction or they just saw easy money.

The admission to a drug and alcohol rehab didn't last long. The first time my siblings and mom visited, my little brother handed me a map. From the backseat of the car he had drawn a map, street names included for how to get to where I was - which he told me proudly, would allow me to walk home following the map backwards. I didn't bother to tell him it wasn't a very realistic idea since walking home would be more than a 40-mile walk. I just loved that he cared.

I had a terrible attitude. I liked the attention that other kids gave me when I acted like I was badass. People just didn't mess with me, and I had been messed with enough in my life. This was the safest way to behave. I decided I was leaving that place after watching another kid walk out the doors. I picked my night and as I was grabbing stuff my roommate said she was going with me. She ran and told her cousin and her boyfriend, and they followed me out the doors. It was a terrible night to choose! It started raining within hours of leaving the facility. Even though it was summer, the rain made it chilly. We also didn't have a plan, and I didn't know the town we were in. Neither did the other kids. We spent the night at a park, under the overhang of the building just outside the bathrooms. It was dark, in a town we didn't know. Truth be told, we were scared. The center called the police, and the next day while sitting at an abandoned property sharing the last cigarette we had, the police came along and picked us up.

Here's a shocker, the rehab center didn't want me back! The police called my mom and she sent my uncle to pick me up. He lectured me the whole way home. I had lost a lot of the respect I had for him when we had first moved up here. Shortly after being here, he told me that my mom and stepfather were talking and if she chose to go back to him I'd have to go back too. I don't know what the goal was for telling me that, but I lost a ton of the respect I'd had for him, it took years before that wound was healed too. I swore I'd never be taken back there. So, his lecture fell on deaf ears. I just looked out the window and couldn't wait to see my boyfriend.

Truth was I was messed up – emotionally and I knew it! I just had no idea how to work through all my feelings and emotions. I didn't like the person I was. I didn't know what was wrong with me. I didn't understand how my trauma had created poor coping skills; I was still in survival mode even though my stepfather wasn't an active part of my life anymore. I didn't understand why everything just didn't get better now that he wasn't here. I did not know why numbing everything felt better, neither did anyone else that was around me. Why couldn't I just be better? Why wasn't I happy? It's what I wanted most.

I sat up at night wondering who the hell I actually was. I didn't know. I was so lost and no one else seemed to have the answers I needed; not counselors, not my boyfriend, not my family. How could I feel better when I didn't understand why I didn't feel fine in the first place, and I didn't know what was causing my unhappiness and behavior. Would I ever be better? Maybe I was completely and totally broken and forever lost.

Creeping

It doesn't matter how far I've run
There is never an escape that brings the sun
Life is always shades of gray
I'm hurt, I'm lonely, I'm alone, and I'm ashamed.

I try to outrun the voice that sounds like his
It lives in my brain, it's stuck in my head
I think I'm better but it only lasts for a while
The colors were beginning to grow bright

Then the grays and blacks descend
Creeping along the edges and then filling everything in
The dread and fear and anger and shame
Come alive again like a creeping pain

Demolishing my efforts, reducing my strides
What does better look like?
I thought I'd figured it out, it's supposed to get easier,
right?
Yet here I go down that slide to hell again!

His voice comes creeping into my dreams
Taking the peace and replacing it with pain
Creeping in and creeping round
I can't break free; I just move on to another round

The darkness stalks me, always lingering near
His words, my fears they all merge
Creating despair and a feeling of loathing
I hate myself and what I've become

The voice echoes in my head
Stalking me, creeping up when I don't expect it
Momentary joy and happiness stolen again
The creeping never seems to end.

When I was younger, I had wanted to be a lawyer, but at this point, I didn't know what I wanted to be other than whole again. I wanted to not constantly hurt. Even when there was a smile on my face there was an underlying hurt that still made its way into everything. I could be having a wonderful time with people and that insidious voice would creep in telling me I'd never be good for anything. I did not want to believe it. I knew it was all some weird aftermath of my abuse; but I didn't understand trauma, and the brain science wasn't out there like it is now to tell me that my brain had been wired a certain way due to trauma. I did not have a clue about the way trauma affected the brain. Later when I learned about it, I felt a lightbulb moment.

My coping skills made me a people pleaser or sometimes I went the opposite way because I felt so much resentment that I'd be a complete jerk to everyone. I didn't have good boundaries. I didn't know how to do normal things or be happy doing normal things; no one told me that many people don't feel fulfilled until they have dealt with their trauma.

I was still dating Bob. He was still there, I hadn't run him off, he hadn't given up. When my uncle took me home, he made me call my mom at work. He left while I spoke to her, and she told me I was to stay home. I agreed but as soon as I hung up the phone I ran up to my room, grabbed a couple of things, then walked across town to where Bob worked. He didn't know I had been kicked out of the rehab center. He wasn't on the floor working yet so I walked in the back and up the stairs to the breakroom. I watched him talking to a co-worker and laughing for almost a full minute before he stopped and turned towards the door as if something had told him to look. His coworker also turned.

He took a few steps across the room to me, grabbing me in an embrace that felt like the best thing I had ever felt. It was a good reunion. He was my safe person, my safe place, which is crazy considering how messed up we both were due to the traumas we had individually experienced. We had a common hurt, we cared deeply about each other, and we held on for dear life, even when our actions were counterproductive to a healthy relationship.

As things would go, I found myself pregnant shortly after returning home. I had morning sickness, but not bad. I vomited on a few occasions but nothing too bad and I convinced myself I must have just been sick. I also could no longer smoke a cigarette first thing in the morning. After missing two periods I knew I had to be pregnant, despite not wanting to be. I did some praying; that 'god is a genie' kind of prayer kids do when they really want something but know it will take a miracle to get it. That didn't work either.

So, I took the test. I didn't have to wait until the timer went off, it was positive. DAMNIT! Now what? I talked to Bob. We decided we were just kids, not even out of high school, we were not ready for a kid, and we knew a couple people who had been pregnant but had given their babies up for adoption and it seemed the kindest, best, and most mature thing we could do was give up the baby. Easy as could be, right? There wouldn't be any regrets, and the baby would have a great family taking care of them. We could get our lives together and figure things out from there. Even after all these years, as I sit here writing this my heart clenches and hurts and tears fill my eyes. As a mother I know that's not how that goes and that my heart would have broken every single day for the rest of my life.

Enter my mom on the scene. I told her one night before she went bowling with her friends. Her best friend was to pick her up and had called saying she was leaving her house and would be there in a few minutes. That gave me about 5 minutes. I waited three minutes. "Mom, I have to tell you something." She was standing in the kitchen putting on her lipstick. She turned. "I'm pregnant. I'm not keeping it. We are putting it up for adoption." Her eyes went wide with shock and then filled with tears. She didn't say anything, just looked at me with those tears forming in her eyes. A car horn honked. She grabbed her things and wiped her eyes; opened the door and told me we would talk later. We didn't talk later that night. I ran out of the house as soon as she got home.

A couple of days later we were driving across town, I still didn't have a car. My mom was looking out the window paying attention to the road. Without looking at me she said "So, you're giving the baby up for adoption?" I said "yes" with no hesitation at all. "Okay, I won't give you any opinion, but I want you to think about something. How will you feel when that little girl or boy turns 8 or 9 or 10 and you start wondering if they are safe, if someone is doing the same thing to them that he did to you? I'd think that would drive a person insane because you'll never know if they are being loved or abused." I immediately felt the pit in my stomach and knew that her words had changed everything. Tears immediately sprung to my eyes. I had been feeling this baby move and I was already starting to feel guilty at the idea of giving him or her up. I didn't need my mom throwing this Portuguese mom guilt at me. What was she doing?

She was a smart woman. She dropped me off at work. When I finished my shift, I went to meet Bob. He worked later than I did. I walked into the aisle he and his co-worker were in. We were all friends. His co-worker saw me before Bob did and knew I wasn't okay. When Bob turned to me and was getting ready to ask if I was okay, I said "I'm not giving this baby up for adoption. I couldn't live with myself not knowing if my baby is safe or not. I can't live with the idea that someone could abuse this child, and I couldn't do anything to save them. You don't have to stay with me. You can go off to school or go to California with the guys in your band. I'm going to stay here and raise our baby. Whether you want to be here or not is your choice. I'll wait for you if you ask me to, but I don't expect you to stay here. Think about it and let me know." I turned on my heel, brave and firm. I didn't want to make him decide now but I also didn't want to look at him in case he said he wouldn't stay. One step, two steps, he grabbed my arm and turned me around pulling me into his arms. "I don't need time to think about it. I love you. I'm not going anywhere."

He was a good guy. He had his own demons and has his own story to tell but that's not mine to share. Despite all his own struggles over the years he has always been there for me. That decision we made, to raise our child together, changed the trajectory of our lives. We went to the community college and took GED classes, graduating two days before our daughter was born.

Cassandra was born May 18, 1992. She was a beautiful, tiny girl who changed our world. She changed mine and continues to do so in the most positive ways.

Words

A simple sentence,
Just a few words
Can change a life's course.

Our words create damage
Firestorms of hurt
That burns someone from the inside.

Our words create joy
An uplifting of the soul
That takes away pain, even for a short time.

The words of a loved one
Can get us through
Carry us past all the darkness our soul has endured.

Words are so simple
Yet so very powerful
Creating, building, tearing-down, or changing our lives.

Choose them wisely
And be careful with another's heart
The bruises they carry are hard to see sometimes.

We had a little family and ten days after Cassandra turned one, we were married. My mom had pushed for this. She had always loved Bob. She thought he was funny, sweet, and despite being a long-haired, heavy metal listening guy she saw what was deep down; a kid who had a really dysfunctional family who just wanted love.

His co-worker and our friend, served as his best man. His girlfriend, my high school friend, was my maid of honor. The entire wedding and reception had been planned in a month. My friend and I had searched for a dress for me. White dresses were not to be found at JCPenney or any of the other department stores in May 1993. We settled on a non-traditional blue dress. It was pretty, and it was the right price, on clearance!

The four of us sat up drinking the night before, pre-gaming, before we knew that was the term. We got up the next day ready to head to the courthouse and get married. It was gray and overcast outside. This made me sad, but my maid of honor insisted everything was going to be perfect. We traveled to the courthouse where we were married in front of about a dozen family members, a few friends, and our daughter.

My mom had booked a room at a local place for us to have our reception. As a single mom she was on a budget and got Bob's parents to agree to help split the costs. The place provided food. Mom had hired a DJ who had a ton of cassettes and records sitting with him. A co-worker of my husband's gave us a wedding cake. My husband's father brought his fancy camera and promised to take pictures of the wedding and reception; most of the pictures were of his new girlfriend dancing. We should have sprung for a photographer!

As we sat at the head table finishing up our dinner, my new sister-in-law walked up and announced, "I don't give this marriage 6 months", laughed and walked away. I sat shocked and on the verge of tears. She had always been this way but on my wedding day it seemed more than cruel. My husband and my friend reminded me that she was who she was (not in those words). My husband reminded me that his sister's own marriage had only lasted a little longer than about six months after her second child was born and she had gone through several boyfriends in the year and a half since that ended.

She had never liked me. The first time I met her, the summer after my freshman year, his family had a cookout. She arrived late; everyone was already eating. She sat down next to me. I smiled and said "Hi, you must be Bob's sister." She gave me a disdainful look, let her eyes slide from my face down and then back to my face and announced loudly so that everyone in attendance could hear "I don't like you, you aren't good enough for my brother." I was still a kid trying to protect myself from harm and I was quick witted enough to respond, "It's a good thing he doesn't need your permission to date me then." This set the tone for our relationship going forward. Sometimes people don't click. That is okay! The people pleaser in me desperately wanted her to like me and I tried for years. She and I would just never click. I recognize now that she too has her own issues and damage.

Despite being very damaged kids who knew nothing about marriage or raising a family we fought through the tough times. We had a strong desire to make our marriage work and despite all our self-sabotaging ways we did love eachother. We both did a lot to sabotage our marriage. The early days of it were brutal with lots of tears, lots of fights that led to him leaving the house for hours. He always came home though. We would cry through explanations and make-up or just carry on as if nothing had happened. Avoidance worked well until all the feelings spilled over and an argument ensued. Neither one of us knew how to be married, how to be healthy individually, and certainly not to be healthy as a couple. Trying to grow up and figure out how to heal from traumas that we didn't even fully understand was not an easy task. People may not have understood our relationship, or the pull we had that kept us together. We didn't either. We just kept showing up and trying hard to make it work.

As bad as that sounds, we also had so many amazing times. We attended concerts; Ozzy Osbourne and Lollapalooza were among the more memorable ones in those early years. We went camping at cheap places so that we'd have adventures. We had big family Sunday dinners. We had a group of friends who would all congregate at our place since we were the first ones to have a proper place. The rule was no drinking until Cassy was asleep and the noise level had to be kept down.

We moved a few times. A couple years into our marriage his mom approached us to purchase her mom and dad's house as her father had just passed away. We had no idea what we were doing. We had already amassed about two thousand dollars in debt, which in the process of things his family loaned us to pay off debt. We had had a car accident prior to this, which was part of the cause of that debt because I hurt my back in the accident and had been off work for a period of time. We paid off the debt and when our settlement came in used it to put down on the house. People just told us what to do but we weren't given explanations for the why behind what we were told. The family decided that the house should be purchased by my husband and his mom without my name on anything. They gave us the reasons for this, something about building our credit and later purchasing it out from his mom. We trusted them. We were young and had no idea about home ownership, no one had ever guided us on what to do. We did what we were instructed to do. I attended the closing and watched as my husband signed the paperwork making him a homeowner.

In the months to come, tension arose. First his mom refused to give us the payment book for the house payments. She then informed us that the house payment had gone up by three hundred dollars a month. I questioned this and she told me to mind my own business as the house wasn't mine anyway. I finally called the mortgage company and got a letter sent to me showing that the payment had not gone up after the closing. I told my husband, expecting him to get angry. Instead, he said his mom had to have a good reason for it. This caused more tension between us and because we were not good at conflict and conversations around that we struggled. She would frequently pop over, unannounced, barging in without knocking. She and I exchanged words about her just walking in without knocking, I was informed her name was on the house not mine. She would leave me notes telling me she and my husband had decided that I needed to do certain things. I wanted out of this mess. Desperately! At one point I did leave and stayed with a friend for a couple of months, but I loved my husband, just not his family, so we got back together.

He did ask her about the letter from the mortgage company. She explained that she had been trying to help us save money by having us pay her the mortgage payment and then putting away money for us as a rainy-day fund. I chimed in "Great. Then give us back the extra money so we can put it in our own bank account." My husband yelled at me to stop. She told me again to mind my own business. Several months later she showed up during her lunch. She had papers in her hands informing my husband that she had received them in the mail from the bank and they needed to be signed. He had just woken up as he worked second shift. He sat down to start signing. We had just had our son, and I was holding him when I said, "Don't you think you should read those before you sign them?" His response "Patty, stop! This is my mom. What's your problem?" She smiled a smug smile at me. He signed the paperwork, and she left.

We got into a fight about what my problem with his mom was. I had a list ready for him and it was a long list that included a lot of finger pointing at him. Despite trying to make everything work we were on the edge of nothing working out. He told me that I was a dead wrong, that his mom wouldn't do anything to screw him over. I mentioned the "rainy day" money and how she hadn't turned that over to us. This fight lasted for hours before he finally said he had to leave for work, which also indicated I needed to walk to our daughter's school and pick her up. The real issue was that neither of us had good boundaries and his mother also did not have good boundaries, nor did she know how to respect the boundaries others tried to put up.

As if that wasn't enough, on top of that he and I did not communicate effectively.

Less than a week later his mom showed up at the house and placed a "For Sale" sign in the front yard, then walked into the house announcing that we needed to find a new place to live. My husband questioned her, not understanding what was happening. I knew though. The papers he had signed had gotten his name off the house somehow. She had taken the house from us. She had done exactly what I had feared when she came into the house with the papers.

We began looking for a new place to live. I was full of resentment, much of it misplaced towards him, and he was also angry at the world, his mom, and at me.

Sabotage

I need you, I love you
But I don't know how to love myself
I keep creating problems
And I don't know how to stop this cycle.

I want a good life
I have what it takes
Things are going good and then
BAM! I'll sabotage it and burn it down.

Reduced to a pile of ashes
I'll try to build it all back up
I want the good life
But I keep setting it on fire.

Why am I like this?
Why can't I do better?
I hate myself and you deserve better.
You should leave, please don't go.

When will enough be enough
And you'll walk away because I'm not worthy of your love
I want to believe that I am but the past tells me different
So, I'll push and I'll push because I can't accept this love.

I am damaged goods, I am a mess
A little girl in a woman's body unable to get it together
The voice in my head tells me it's all going to go up in
flames
I'd rather burn it myself than have you not love me.

It makes no sense. I don't want you to leave
But I sabotage myself, my life, our happiness.
A cycle that never stops, a crazy loop that I can't get out of
Love and pain, tears and fights

It makes no sense
Why am I like this?
I want it all but don't believe I can have it.
His words whisper in my head.

Unlovable, worthless, stupid, and no-good
I hate his voice, and I hate his hold on me
How can I stop it,
Why can he still control me?

Sabotage; it happened again
When things are good
I just can't believe it
So, I create the flame and cry myself to sleep

Prove him wrong and love me
No matter what I do
Prove me wrong and show me
A better way.

Sabotage is an ugly truth
Trauma creates it
Because we don't see our worth
Stop asking why there is no easy answer.

Healing means confronting
The things I hate about me and the reason I hate me
Healing means working through
What happened to me?

Healing is hard, even when you understand what's creating the issues! Our twenties were filled with self-destructive habits, followed by arguments, and shutting the other out. Blame was thrown around like gifts at a talk show. We were destructive to ourselves and to each other! We were both trying to love each other, but neither of us could quite love ourselves.

We had our daughter, another son and then we had a set of twins. They were three months premature. This was followed by a lengthy hospital stay and even after they were home, years of doctors' appointments, specialists, early intervention, surgeries, IEP's, 501's, and struggles.

Neither of us managed these things well. We did not have many people around us who guided us. Instead, it felt like there was so much undermining that took place. One of us would confide in someone but then it only served to stir the pot. That person stirred the pot, the situation stirred the pot, we stirred the pot. We were both just two damaged people, set on some kind of self-destruction, pointing fingers at each other, not being particularly good to one another and not giving ourselves or each other the grace to get better, yet we kept hanging on. Somewhere deep inside we both believed we could fix ourselves and each other. The problem was we each knew we were a problem, contributing to the struggles our marriage faced. We both wanted to show up better, but we self-sabotaged and in the process hurt each other.

Who had time to work on themselves and get better when we were just struggling to survive? My husband had plant shutdowns, we had ups and downs, financially we were a disaster. Neither of us was willing to point a finger at ourselves during an argument because we both moved in defensiveness. 'I did this because you did that.'

How we made it through is something I don't spend too much time considering; luck, grace, a higher power and plan, stubborn determination, being terrified of going it alone…I just don't know but I'm glad we are on the other side of so many of those things. There were a lot of lies; to ourselves and to each other. There was pain, resentment, and loathing; both created by each of us hurting ourselves and hurting each other. We just couldn't see it all clearly. We knew the other was upset or suffering and yet, when asked we'd both say we were fine, and nothing was wrong. We had learned to avoid hard conversations. That was something we excelled at, we would just sweep it under the rug and carry on! Vulnerability and truth led to pain, and we avoided that at all costs. Our lives growing up had created that understanding. We had to protect ourselves with defensiveness. If this life we shared was painful it would be far more painful if we were vulnerable and had hard conversations…. right?

During those years, I tried to be seen as perfect. Perfectly in control, perfectly adjusted, perfectly sensible, perfectly married, perfectly happy, a perfect parent. I struggled and somewhere in the back of my mind I knew that I needed to get better; for myself, my children, and my husband.

Phantom

The eyes are a window to the soul, they say
What is it you find when you look inside mine
A smile that never reaches my eyes
The sparkle was lost a long time ago
Hidden emotions pushed deep within
Fear that cannot be seen
But which terrorizes me day and night
Shame for the things
I could not prevent
And for the things
I have allowed
Do you think you see the real me
No, you simply see the phantom
The ghost of who I should have been
The camouflage I wear
Like a second skin
So that when you look
You see what you wish to see.

In my early thirties things settled down a bit. I thought things were better. We both had decent jobs, ones that were not just jobs, but we considered as long-term careers. The twins were in school and past the years of medical emergencies and therapies for development. We hadn't had a major fight in a while.

Then things became uncomfortable again. My husband was always sleeping. I was sure he was depressed or on drugs. He'd barely get up to go to work. One day at work I got a call from his boss asking if he was okay because he hadn't been at work all week and no one had heard from him. I was confused. Where could he be? I left work and drove home. I found him asleep on our bed. I woke him up, asking him what his problem was. Where had he been going every morning? None of this was done in a kind and loving manner that gave room for explanation. It was accusatory. I was concerned. I was also annoyed and angry. We were never quite out of the woods and financially comfortable plus why had he been lying to me about going to work?

I found out that he had been leaving and going down the road and sitting in his truck until I left the house with the kids and headed to work, then he was driving home and going back to bed. He said he could hardly stay awake. He was just exhausted. I was far from amused. I was angry. I was worried about him, about us keeping a roof over our heads, about how I'd make up the money, I was frustrated that he hadn't told me something was going on. I had a lot of feelings, but I couldn't create a pause and consider what all those emotions did to me and how I showed up for him. "What the fuck is wrong with you?" I screamed. He answered that he didn't know. I took this as him just not caring. I told him that before I got home, he needed to make some choices. I gave him an ultimatum.

1. Call a doctor and get an appointment to find out what was wrong.
2. Call a counseling center and get in to them to figure out what was wrong in his head.
3. Pack a bag and move out.

I was a mess and went back to work. Later I got a call from him asking who our family physician was. He made an appointment. I was not showing up with love. I was showing up with resentment, and frustration, and felt so uncertain about everything that I just did not know how to show up well. I wanted to believe I was showing up with love and concern because that was what I felt but given the uncertainty and my need for certainty I showed up stressed out and frustrated. Over the years I have been able to look back and see how I didn't give grace, I was overwhelmed and lashed out and I certainly didn't create a safe place in our marriage for him to be genuine, honest, and vulnerable. I was functioning in survival mode, in fight mode and it showed up in how I engaged.

At around this same time, our daughter, starting her senior year in high school, announced she was pregnant. We were at church, the kids and I, when she made this announcement just as the service started. I don't have a clue what the sermon was about. To this day I can't recall anything other than her words, barely audible, a whisper really, repeated in my head for the entire hour. She leaned over and whispered "I'm pregnant" just as the priest began mass. She then looked forward and never moved for the remainder of mass. Our priest still laughs about this to this day.

The following week we got into doctors and found out that she was six months pregnant. This does not leave a lot of time for putting everything in place. We talked to the school, and she had enough credits to graduate in December after the first semester. To her this would be a nightmare, she was in A'Cappella and other activities. We decided she would do her birth-related leave at home with a tutor provided from the school, return to school in the spring, and she would graduate in May with the rest of her class.

My husband's mother ranted and raved that we needed to make her drop out of school to get her G.E.D. and a job to support herself, just like she had done, just like her daughter had done. One of her favorite sayings was "It was good enough for (Insert me, her, her daughter) so it's good enough for (insert her, you, them)." This applied to spankings, working in factories instead of going to college, and getting pregnant as a teenager. We ignored her advice. We ended all conversation around the subject and simply moved forward.

My coworker helped plan Cassy's baby shower. She did more of the work than anyone else. I was walking around stressed and panicked, dealing with this situation and wondering what the heck was happening with my husband. The baby shower the same day my husband had his doctor's appointment. He wasn't at the baby shower. I was angry. I needed him to just show up and be supportive. I walked outside and called. Furious and frustrated and overwhelmed. He told me he was on his way but that the doctor had said he believed he had some type of lymphoma and that he had to go get some additional tests. A year before I had seen our family doctor who thought I also had lymphoma. I went for a bunch of tests and there was no lymphoma. I flippantly replied to my husband with "He loves to say people have lymphoma."

He showed up at the very end of the party, We were already cleaning up. He was preoccupied with his own stuff, his own new worries, or the news he had been expecting but hadn't felt comfortable talking with me about. I was tired, overwhelmed, and mad at him. I didn't even consider what he might have been feeling at that moment. I was too worried about all the things on my plate. Again, I wanted him to show up better for me, without realizing that he likely needed the same from me and I was failing miserably.

In a matter of weeks, we saw several doctors: the primary, an ENT, an Oncologist. He had several appointments and then got the call for us both to show up at the doctor's office. We drove separately, wrapped up in our own thoughts. The doctor confirmed the original suspicions were true. It was cancer. It was Non-Hodgkin's Lymphoma. We left the appointment, shocked. He went to visit his mom. I went to the gas station and bought a pack of cigarettes. Despite having quit several years before this was the most overwhelming news that I could imagine, and I needed the calming effect that pulling a drag off a cigarette and releasing it allowed me.

I stood on the back porch. Crying. Tears falling. I called my mom. It was a short call. I then called my little brother. I remember after telling him that my husband had cancer "I don't know how to fix this. How do I fix this?" That summed up a lot of my own damage. When I had people and things to fix, I functioned well. I was a fixer. I did not have to explore my own damage, my own behaviors, or address my trauma when I was so busy fixing everyone and everything in the world around me. I registered that comment as important. I remember thinking it was telling and that it needed to be examined...but not right now, right now there was fixing to do!

So began chemo followed by radiation. He went to a dark place; he was alone and I didn't make him feel less alone. I tried, but I showed up the way I thought I should, without asking him how he needed me to show up for him. I babied him, I took care of him physically but emotionally he was as alone as I usually felt. I didn't know how to reach him, and my efforts fell short. I didn't recognize that either. I didn't understand why he struggled and didn't open up to me like I so badly wanted him to. I just always knew there was a part of him he kept locked up.

These things are more easily recognizable now as being issues we both struggled with. We both always felt alone despite the efforts of the other to connect, to show love and support. It was a long reaching effect of our childhood trauma's; we just had no real understanding around it, and no one was sharing the connection about childhood trauma and the way the brain then develops. We were two lost souls struggling to survive. Struggling to live, struggling to parent, struggling to make this marriage work, and struggling to survive this crisis. So frequently what we want is not in line with how we show up. How we show up results in the opposite effect than what we desire most.

Our grandson was born early in my husbands' treatment, at the end of October. That little boy was the connection of love my husband needed and didn't even know he needed. I don't know that without our grandson and the bond my husband immediately felt with him that he'd have fought like he did to make it through treatments that wrecked his body, which left him weak, sick, and exhausted.

Just a couple of weeks shy of a full year after treatments started, he finished his last radiation treatment. We celebrated with a trip to the Indy 500. I had purchased tickets from a friend who was selling a set very cheap. We had an amazing weekend. He was finished with treatment. I foolishly thought things would be better now. I still didn't see that a traumatic event doesn't just end and magically life gets better. If only that were the case. Situations, events, trauma all change us. It changes us, it changes the people we love, it changes the perspectives we have and therefore things do not just go back to normal. Often, we so desperately want to believe that the end of a crisis or situation will result in things going back to normal, but we are changed forever by the crisis or situation and need to adjust to a new normal.

My husband decided to go back to school to get his certification as a mechanic. He had wanted to do this since high school. After our high school graduation his aunt had asked what was next for him and he responded, "I think I'll go to the community college to get my degree in auto mechanics." He had not taken that path though. He had been dissuaded from doing so by his family, however, it had always been something he had wanted to do. This second chance at life seemed like the perfect time to get serious about pursuing his passion.

I one hundred percent wanted him to go back to school, to support him as he pursued his dream. I did not realize that as he did so, we hadn't talked about how it would look, or expectations around school and work, so instead of being able to show up with full support, I harbored some resentment as I continued to work multiple jobs to support our family as he went to school. The power and absolute need for having difficult conversations was something neither of us understood or knew how to begin. It was something we had learned wasn't safe to do when we were children and we both avoided those conversations with every ounce of power we possessed.

In the moment, I would have said that I had things figured out. I had done work on myself (that wasn't untrue), I had a good job, I had a healthy family, I had a grandson who lit up our world. I had it together. I was adulting and life was fine! In truth, all that childhood trauma was showing up in ways that made me show up as less than the best version of myself!

Life continued. My husband graduated from college and got a job. He then moved to a shop that gave him more opportunities for learning. After about a year there he had the opportunity to interview for a job with a locally owned shop, one he would feel proud to work at. He was offered the job following his interview and has been there since.

I had also landed a job with a local family-owned company. I was proud to work there. This family cared about its employees. That was very different from the work setting I had just left. Things were looking better. As it were, we both landed at family-owned companies with owners who lived the things they said and cared deeply about the well-being of their employees.

We both realized we had so much work to do. We realized we needed to start recognizing and then working through our triggers, changing the way our pain and suffering had shaped us and retrain our brains and how we reacted. We had to recognize that we were toxic to people around us far too frequently. We needed to learn new coping skills. We needed to learn to communicate. We had to be able to stop ourselves when triggered and utilize new tools to effectively move forward without carrying on those self-sabotaging reactions. We needed to do some hard work on ourselves, our marriage, and our parenting skills.

Scars

Self-Assessment - I am filled with scars
Some you'll see and some you'll find only in the history I
tell
A surgeon's work - the scar line faint as the years have
gone by
Chicken pox scars, a line on my head where hair won't
grow,
A scar from learning to shave my legs
All faint lines now as time has gone by
No pain associated with them anymore
They can be touched and poked - I'll not feel a thing.

The scars you don't see cause far more harm
The pain still resonates and causes memories to flood my
brain
Words used to harm; to undermine, to intimidate
Smells that trigger the remembrance of those moments are
not lost to time
They come in unexpectedly, in a store while passing a
stranger
Or in moments of joy when suddenly the dark veil falls and
steals the smile from my face
Those scars can be dealt with in so many ways - often the
coping brings about more pain
To learn to deal with them appropriately one must stand
firm and acknowledge them

"Hey you, I see you, I know you, I feel you, you live in me
I can't banish you to the depths of hell, you've become as
much a part of me as my skin
Living and breathing and taking up space; space in my
mind given rent free

But I understand you now, I know why you're here, I'm still me and I carry you
You're part of my story, part of my strength, a sign of resilience in the face of pain
As long as I breathe I know you'll remain but I know you and I see you
And I'll give you your space. I'll acknowledge you and breathe through and lean on
Every lesson I've learned to keep you from stealing the life that I've built."

I know the scars and recognize the triggers they cause
I can see them; an obstacle in my day and in my life
I know how to move now I've learned a great deal
Healing doesn't erase the scar but it does reduce the pain
I've learned to carry on, to hope and dream and build what I want
I've learned to hold onto love given and trust it
The healing comes slowly, building on triumphs over the pain that tries to steal my joy
My scars are part of me and I have survived and learned to thrive.

Being busy always seemed like the best idea. Being busy meant I wasn't lazy. Being busy meant I had commitments and a lot of stuff happening in my life. Being busy allowed me an excuse to not sit quietly with my thoughts for too long. My downtime was filled with noise. As long as the silence didn't set in, things were okay.

I had a side business, I worked full time, I sometimes worked multiple jobs, I volunteered. I was a parent, I was a wife, I was a grandma. In those downtime minutes I read books, I got lost in music, or I enjoyed the argumentative nature that social media can take when controversial subjects and opinions mix. I didn't see this as bad. I saw it as being busy, being vocal, being engaged.

Busyness is an avoidance tactic. I was great at using this tactic without ever having realized that it was how I was functioning, and, in the process, I was avoiding having to deal with my trauma. I stayed busy. I helped other people - another avoidance factor; the more people you are helping with their own issues and difficulties and unhealed issues - the less time you must consider your own issues.

After I began working for this company, I started to recognize more of my toxic behaviors. Toxic to myself, toxic to those around me, toxic to the people who were on the receiving end of my behaviors. In a discussion about the ACE indicators someone in my company mentioned that none of those applied to them. They had a zero score. I, on the other hand, had a solid nine, possibly ten if you accepted the couple of nights here or there that my stepfather spent quietly in jail to "Cool down" without any actual charges being filed. By all indications, I was supposed to be a mess. I felt good that I was a parent, with a marriage that had lasted, with long-term friendships, and a steady job. I did not have addiction issues. I was not the mess that test indicated I should be.

But that wasn't completely true. I was a walking disaster who portrayed things as being just fine.
We know that if we want to learn and get better, we should surround ourselves with people who are educated in that area, who are knowledgeable resources for us. We also have often heard that who you surround yourself with will define who you are. The people I worked for made me very aware of where I was missing the mark. They made me want to be better, show up better, and help others. I realized to help anyone else, I needed to help myself first.

I began reading more books about healing. I had started community college years before and had quit. Being successful with school was scary and I always said life got in the way - the kids, their needs, but the truth was success meant something and deep down I didn't believe I deserved it nor that I was good enough to have it. More self-sabotaging and limiting behavior.

I realized I was a busy, perfectionist, who loved being brutally honest with others while self-sabotaging myself and using excuses for why I was allowed a pass. What I realized was that I was still a mess. I wasn't all that much better, or at least not as much as I wanted to be.

The truth was I was better than I had been 20 years before, but I still had a long way to go. Why couldn't I just set this all aside and move on and be totally happy?

I knew these truths when the silence descended or went on for too long. I hated myself in so many ways for how hard I tried to be okay but couldn't quite get it right, which just fueled my belief that I didn't deserve happiness that lasted.

What was wrong with me? Why couldn't I just get it right?

Devour

This darkness that surrounds me
Always threatens to pull me down
It's hungry mouth desires to devour
All that I've worked so hard to gain

The happiness I feel
Is nothing more than fleeting
It careens into the pit
The haze is just too thick

Something is wrong with me
Joy I cannot find
Heart and soul filled
With shadows and holes

Rage and hatred
Hurt and disgust
These things overpower
The small glimpses of hope

Save me from myself
From the destruction
That comes from inside
Save me before time runs out

Something has to change
Something has to give
Or else
How can I continue to live?

The mind does interesting things and works against you sometimes. I had seen and experienced it firsthand. The voice of my stepfather ringing in my head when I was succeeding, telling me I didn't deserve it, I was a fraud, I was not good enough. Why couldn't I silence him?

My daughter became involved with a company that has a retreat for women who are survivors of childhood sexual abuse. She told me about it. She told me I should apply to go. I looked it up. It looked like opening a can of worms that I didn't want to deal with. It also looked like something I really wanted and needed to do.

I filled out an application at the urging of my daughter. The retreat was free. FREE? Who does that? The retreat was in the mountains of Utah and you had to pay for your trip there. I still had some kids at home, and despite being accepted I told my daughter I just couldn't really justify spending the money on airfare. The next thing I knew she had put the word out and got the money together to send me. Her best friend jumped in to help. Several of my friends jumped in to put money towards my trip. They all realized how my trauma affected me and that this was an opportunity I should take rather than passing pu.

In October 2017 I got dropped off at O'Hare International Airport and jumped on a flight headed west. The first leg of the flight stopped in Las Vegas. I was the only person who stayed on the plane. I contemplated getting off the plane and hanging out in Vegas for four days. I could just tell everyone I went to the retreat, and no one would ever know differently. *'What the hell had I been thinking?'* I asked myself. I didn't want to go talk about my abuse. I didn't want to relive it with a bunch of other women in who knows what kind of mental space. My nerves were getting the best of me. My palms were sweating, I was nervous, and I was on an airplane, a tin box in the sky, heading towards something unknown, uncomfortable, and terrifying - to talk about my pain, my trauma and the shame I felt deeply and could not shake.

The paperwork I had received talked about how we would not have cell phone service the whole time. I didn't really know how comfortable I was with that. I certainly didn't like the idea of being disconnected. There was an emergency number that I gave my husband so he could reach me but that was only for emergencies. We were able to use the housephone there, but the time was very limited. We were working on us and outside distractions were not allowed.

I arrived at Salt Lake City airport, which was very busy. I found my way to the doors where I was to be picked up. I went outside and chain smoked. One more poor coping skill I had acquired over the years. I went back inside and found a corner to sit in. The corner was protected space, if someone was going to come my way I'd see them, they couldn't sneak up. I pondered this tas I sat there, texting my husband and my friend who I had only recently found out had attended the same retreat. I questioned my mental ability to manage whatever was coming my way. I realized even while sitting and waiting I tried to guard and protect myself (thus sitting in a corner).

I watched as people congregated near the exit, waiting for their rides. A few women I pegged immediately as going to the retreat. One stood out, her black hair, her heeled boots, her confident stance despite only being about 5 foot tall. I knew immediately she was one of them, one of us,

156

one of the women I'd be spending this week with. I was drawn to her and terrified of her. I didn't know why, but I knew she was either going to be someone I could not stand or someone I loved; there wasn't going to be anything in between.

The counselors showed up. Signs with initials on them indicating that they were there to pick us up without announcing to others the reason we were all gathered. We were moved into groups and walked out to SUV's. I sat in the back. I watched as the black-haired girl jumped up front to ride shot gun with the counselor. She talked the whole way up the mountain, and I honestly wanted to sit in silence and try to calm my nerves. I sent a text to my friend before we got into the mountains, and I lost service telling her that I didn't think I could do this and telling her about the black-haired girl who just kept talking. A response came quickly to walk my journey and to not worry about what other people were doing on their journey. Solid advice. The whole way up the mountain I just kept thinking '*What have you gotten yourself into*? Here is where the decision was made to step away from comfort, and step into courage (Thanks Brene' Brown!).

We made it up the mountain after a long, beautiful, and noisy ride (the black-haired girl really did talk the whole trip). The mountains were beautiful. I was awestruck. I wanted to climb one and sit on top and just get lost in the beauty. I had never been in the mountains before. I was shocked by the size of the place we were staying. It was a mansion! There were different areas, and we were moved into smaller groups. I walked up the stairs to figure out who my roommate was and who the room next to us would be occupied by as we shared a bathroom.

My roommate was spunky. I adored her immediately. She had an infectious and beautiful smile that lit up the room. The black-haired girl was in the adjoining room, along with another blonde girl who seemed very reserved and as uncomfortable as I was. I liked her! We started talking and in a brief time we were all pals. Our common situation, our nerves, our reservations were all so similar. We were a well-paired foursome that occupied the upstairs corner rooms.

We were introduced to our counselors; we were introduced to everyone. We had a schedule. We had a chef. We explored the grounds, we made friends, we went to sessions that first day I was shocked by how many women talked almost immediately about their abuse, their triggers, their concerns, many of us remained quiet, absorbing it all, assessing those around us, trying to figure out how we fit in, and worrying that we were in over our heads. We were women of all ages, with a lifetime of pain and suffering that many others could not understand, and that sometimes we didn't understand. We were being introduced to the program, the counselors. Staff explained boundaries and how they ensured the safety and well-being of everyone.

We learned about brain science; how early childhood trauma creates connections in the brain that lead to impulsive behaviors, self- sabotaging behaviors, sleep disorders, anxiety disorders, eating disorders and the struggles we had been dealing with all our adult lives. This brain connection information resonated deeply with me. Other women here had similar coping skills, poor coping skills, poor boundaries, and years of shame that pushed constantly against any progress we tried to make.

There were two group counseling sessions that we attended down the mountain. We went in the SUV's and headed down the mountain where we arrived at a huge open spaced building to attend the group counseling sessions. The reason for this was to keep this heavy and deep work off the mountain retreat. The first session kicked my butt. I sat there listening to other women talk about the lack of support they had received. I heard about mothers who didn't believe them, siblings who turned against them, families that called them liars and left them feeling alone and alienated. There were women who hadn't even told their spouses about their abuse. I sat there struggling. What was wrong with me? Why did I struggle so much with my abuse when I had so much support compared to so many of these women? I had a husband who had sat through court with me. I had a mom who left as soon as she knew about the abuse. I had friends who had supported me and stayed by my side through it all. I realized how lucky I was. We are often very caught up in our own issues and struggles but if given the chance to exchange those with others, we would most often decide to keep the struggles and burdens we carry.

We loaded back into the SUV and started heading back up the mountain. I sat there thinking about this and wondering why I couldn't just move forward when I had support that these other women didn't ever have. I began questioning if my being here had kept some other woman who didn't have support from attending. By the time we got about halfway up the mountain I was bawling...I was sobbing. Taking huge gasping breaths, I tried to calm down which only made it worse. My poor new friends in the SUV worried about me and I was unable to do anything but shake my head and sob. I was ugly crying. I grabbed my cigarettes and lighter and went to the side of the house when we returned. Still crying, still struggling with whether I should be here.

My roommate and the two girls from the other room came out to check on me. I tried to explain. They talked to me a bit before going back inside. One of the counselors came out and talked to me. I was chain smoking. I was shaking. I probably had snot on my face. I was a mess. I felt guilty for being there because someone else definitely needed this more than I did. I was a selfish, stupid woman who had it so much better than other people. The counselor let me say all these things and then she said "Patty, were you sexually abused as a child?" I looked at her and nodded, she quietly but firmly said "Then you belong here. You didn't steal someone else's spot. You are a survivor of childhood sexual abuse, and you belong here, you deserve to be here because you deserve to heal. You don't have to feel shame for taking up the space you need to work on healing." I began crying again. This time it was with relief. I did belong here. I didn't need to feel this guilt I was feeling. This counselor addressed something I had struggled with for years now; permission to take space, to be in the room, to belong.

There was a shift. I felt it. I felt it and I recognized it. I was enough; the way I was. I was enough, as I worked towards being better. I deserved a space at this table because I deserved the chance to work on myself, get professional support, and heal. The Maya Angelou quote about doing the best you can until you know better and then you do better, comes to mind. It came to mind then as I felt this shift occur. I was at this place where I could learn the why's of how I felt, why I did what I did, and why I respond the way I do. Once I knew better how to deal with what had happened to me and how it made me feel, I could do better going forward. This was the simplicity and the complexity of this retreat.

There isn't a switch and then everything goes away. There isn't a moment where you heal and boom, the past no longer comes up. The counselors warned us about this. They said that people leave feeling good and then get back home to reality, and family, and stressors and do a back slide. I was prepared for that, and I wasn't going back to being that woman anymore...I wasn't going to live in that place anymore. I was determined. I knew I'd have bad days, but I also realized giving a space to those triggers made them easier to deal with and by creating the space to feel those things, I would be allowing that hurt child that I had been the grace and compassion to heal.

A change was on the horizon.

VOICE

I scream inside my head
The frustration, the need,
Almost more than I can bear

Sitting quietly
So no one will stare
I can feel my blood pumping

Injustice has laid my soul bare
Stripped of so many things
Except the ability to care

Years of shame
Grinding to a halt
I'm healing and you should be scared

I'm growing, I'm healing
I won't continue to be silenced
There is a need to get loud

To speak my truth
To make you uncomfortable
The need rises up as desperate as my need for air

They choked me to silence me
Too loud, too much of everything
But too much is simply your comfort zone being pushed

I don't need to squeeze into your four walls
Because my pain needs release
It's too large to be contained

My voice once silenced
Begins as a whisper
And then starts to boom

Too much, too loud
Too everything for those with no understanding
My voice makes them uncomfortable

But I don't need to ask for forgiveness
Nor can I be silenced again
My voice has been found

The funny thing about healing, like grief, is that the emotions and memories sometimes flood over you unexpectedly. We cannot hold the belief that we will turn a corner, and this will never kick our butts again; it will! We are not left unscathed by the things that have happened to us. We can learn, we can grow, we can work on ourselves, and we can heal. Healing doesn't look like a return to who we were and how we felt before the abuse. We have lost that innocence; we have lost pieces of ourselves to whatever happened to us. Like the loss of a loved one or the birth of a child, we can never return to before that event happened, the experience becomes part of our story, part of our growth, part of our being. Understanding and accepting that are difficult but necessary.

The healing process is a move towards being better. To take the harm that happened to us and create a space to reflect on it, a place to grow from it. I hate when people say that their abuse made them strong. I was strong. I was always strong. I had mental fortitude. I had to use that mental fortitude to live through years of physical, mental, and sexual abuse at the hands of an adult I should have been able to trust. The abuse perpetrated against me did not make me stronger; it broke me into a thousand pieces and because I was strong, I was able to pick those pieces up and continue. I know that the love I felt as a young child prior to my stepfather coming into my life created a resilience in me for which I am so very thankful. Healing is being able to understand the feelings you have, understand, and recognize your triggers, giving yourself permission to put down the armor and let go of our shame. Healing is permission to be who we authentically are, at our core. Healing is an acceptance of the things you cannot go back and change. In life, there are no do-overs, so we must accept the truth that we cannot go back and create a different outcome to the events that already happened.

As a teenager, just out of that situation I did all of this poorly. The damage to me was extreme. I was still strong, but I was in survival mode. No one would hurt me. I chose what happened to me. I also made a lot of poor choices because I didn't know how to love myself or see worth in myself outside of my abuser and the things he had said and done to me.

As a young adult I still struggled. I still struggle today. There are times when I have to put everything down and focus on self-care. There are times that despite my strength and ability to keep moving when the going is tough, I need to lay down my burden for an hour and take care of myself. I will simply tell my spouse that I need a break. I will run a hot bath, sometimes pour a glass of wine or drink a cup of coffee, turn on music that makes me happy and light a candle. Sitting in the tub I have time to think about what is causing the inner turmoil I feel. Or I may jump on my motorcycle and go for a ride, the open air, the sounds, and smells create a space to let it process and then let it go. I can figure out why something is triggering me. I can acknowledge that the pain is there, and I can work through it and offer myself love. At other times people will notice me tapping my chest, this is a grounding tool I have used for years, even before knowing what it was called. It was a soothing method and it serves to bring me back to center.

Someone once told a story about being in a crowd and losing one of their children. They found a police officer, who got on the radio and said they had found the child's parents. An officer came over and handed them their child and they cried with relief. I hadn't had a single thought of my stepfather that day, maybe not even in weeks. That story triggered tears. I felt like I couldn't breathe. I got up and walked to the bathroom at work and sat and cried. I cried for the little girl who got accused of trying to scare everyone and was confused. I cried for the little girl who had just needed the adults in her life to hug her because she was so scared from having been lost. I cried for the little girl who was beaten that night so long ago because she didn't deserve it. She should have been loved and cherished. I cried for joy because I was able to love my children like I hadn't felt loved. I cried for joy because my husband loved our children. I cried because not everyone sucks. I cried because another child who got lost didn't face the same fate that I had. I didn't go down the path of self-destruction. I didn't try to ignore the pain when it came or the grief. I knew that it was okay to let myself feel the emotions, to let them wash over me, to examine them and the reason they created the response and then I was able to step back into my day once all those emotions settled in and I recognized them for what they were, acknowledging them and then moving beyond them.

After the retreat I enrolled in community college for the first time in so many years. I took the couple classes I needed to transfer into a university and to finish my associate's degree. I graduated with honors with my husband, oldest son, daughter in law, and granddaughter watching me. An associates degree might not seem huge to some people although I'd argue that it's a step to be celebrated. I had told myself stories about how I didn't deserve it, how I wasn't smart enough, how I would never make it anywhere. I had self-sabotaged for so many years but now I reached and succeeded. I crossed that stage with pride. It was an achievement that was hard earned; not because college work was difficult for me, in fact, I thrived there but because I had also spent many years feeling like I didn't deserve so many things, especially the good things I wanted. Now I walked across that stage believing I was enough and even if I never did anything else with that degree, I had accomplished it. It was a proud moment in my life.

Since then, I've continued to work on myself, my education, improving how I show up. I've taken more courses, I have read countless books, I have spent hours in conversations with my children and my spouse about how I had failed to show up the way they needed me to at times. I have apologized for mistakes I've made; because they deserved the apology, and I needed to forgive myself for not being able to show up better because of my own unhealed trauma and the things I didn't know.

I have cried, I have journaled, I have written poetry. I have fought anxiety and depression and the desire to portray perfection and learned to be honest with myself and those around me. Some days I'm not okay and that is okay. I can see it, know it and do what I need to do to get through. I've stopped apologizing for feeling, for struggling, for not having the answers and instead I get vulnerable and ask for help more often than ever before. I also have an amazing group of people in my life who support me. A husband who has known me and loved me since I was a damaged and angry teenager. Four children who mean the world to me. Grandchildren who make my days bright. Siblings who love me and who I know I can turn to when everything hits the fan or when I just need to sit and laugh a lot. A best friend who has known me since childhood and loved and supported me despite my self-sabotaging behavior. I am so lucky to have such an amazing group of people in my life who never walk away from me or lose their faith in me. They loved me when I was not very lovable.

I come back to the question and the title of this book so often...'When will she be better?' The answer is always and never. It depends on what you are looking for. She will always be working on healing; it's the natural way our survival brain is programmed. Our bodies want to heal, to be better. She will never be better if your definition is for her to be like she was before. It's an impossible thought process that is filled with potholes and a lot of self-loathing.

There are moments that sneak up and hurt and there are moments where the joy takes away all the shadows. The grief and hurt don't mean that I'm not better, the harm done to me still exists, the pain resides in me and will accompany me throughout my life. That hurt doesn't go away to never return. That's okay. I sit with that inner little girl now when she needs me, and I know that her name is grief. I also know that she sees me today and is in awe of who I've become, and she is proud of me.

I graduated with my Bachelor of Science in Social Work. Flying to my university and walking for graduation was a huge moment for me. A final piece to the journey that took a long time to complete. Where the next years take me, who knows? I plan to continue to learn, to grow, to consider, to accept, to heal, and most of all to love.

I was also given the opportunity this year, to travel to Portugal, to the islands where my family is from. I got to meet my father. I was able to meet him where he is, to accept his explanations, to understand that he made the decisions that made the most sense for his own very personal reasons at that time. I was able to offer my love and forgiveness. I gained new insight. I realized that I had dreamt of this moment for so many years and what I wanted was acceptance. I realized that accepting myself was the most vital and significant thing I could do. We all struggle so deeply with so many issues, that's just simply life, we do not get out of it unscathed in one way or another.

Life is too short to hold these deeply embedded hurts, allowing them to drive us down paths of self-sabotage and pain. Let them go; life becomes so much more, in every possible way, when we do. I am better when I show up with love. My journey has brought me to this place, to this space and I belong here. I am acutely aware of that. I am proud of who I am today. I accept that I have made tremendous mistakes in my past. I accept that I did the best I could with the knowledge I had and as I've grown and learned and healed, I've learned to do better.

Keep healing and don't give up - I promise, it's worth it!

Recognize Me

I was so young,
so vulnerable.
The crimes you committed
Created a self loathing
A pitiful young girl
So unsure of herself
So consumed by fear, anxiety, and pain

Years have passed
A new life has been created
One that I love
One that has been built on the
Patience, kindness, and love
I gifted myself

You caused my spirit to bend and almost break
A wounded being
Because of your sick pleasures
But I put her back together
Mended her pieces
And now if you saw me
You wouldn't recognize me anymore.

I survived, I healed
I created a life and legacy
Of children and grandchildren
Of laughter and hope
Of passion and learning
I was stronger than you, better than you
I was just unable to see that for a long time.

But here I am standing tall

Changing the world one interaction at a time
Helping others find their peace
Because monsters don't get to win
They bully the weak
Until the weak recognize their strength.
No, you wouldn't recognize me anymore

Thank you for joining me as I told my story. I pray that someone who picks this up sees themselves in a new light and recognizes that they can rise above everything and come out on the other side working towards and being the best person they can be. I hope it brings hope.

I hope that through the work I've done, I can show up better for those around me and those I meet. My hope is that every person can find the strength to believe in themselves, to work hard at healing and to show up better for themselves and those around them. The work is hard, it is raw, it will hurt, and it will be difficult, but I promise that coming to the other side is life-changing in the best possible way!

I want to make it clear that I am also one hundred percent aware that I was the villain in someone else's story. I learned that my words could cut and make people stay away from me. I struggled to trust people and I still desperately wanted to be liked and loved. I didn't show up well for people who did show up for me. I was a mess, and I liked myself less and less. One thing about our journey is that we are not always the victim, we are often the villain, and we hurt others because of our hurt.

Seek the resources and the help that you need. They are everywhere. Believe in yourself – you are so strong and so capable and did not deserve the things done to you that caused you harm. There is no single path to healing, we each have to find our way, find the things that help us, but with all learning, we gain understanding, insights, knowledge, and add new tools to our toolbox that allow us to properly approach the challenges we face in our journey. Find a support system, sometimes that is not friends and family, I hope that you find an amazing group of people to support you, because going it alone is difficult. Support can be your counselors, a group of individuals who have shared experiences, or just those individuals who show up with love and understanding.

Always remember, you are deserving of good things!

There are so many people to thank, and I will feel bad for forgetting people if I don't name them all.

So, I'll keep it simple: I am grateful for each person who has helped me and walked beside me or encouraged me over the years.

I particularly need to thank my mom, who never doubted the truth of what happened and who did all the uncomfortable things to get us to a safe place.

My husband, who has been at my side through all the craziness, has stepped into both my struggles and my healing journey with full engagement and support.

My best friend of 45 years who is the biggest hype-person ever and has always just wanted my safety and my happiness.

My children who might be my biggest cheering section. My siblings and my friends, my co-workers, and so many others who push me out of my comfort zones, who cheer for me when I get uncomfortable and who push me to keep reaching for the next thing. They make me laugh and feel loved when things feel like they are falling apart. They make me a better person and they believe in me when I struggle to believe in myself.

I am truly blessed and grateful.

Made in United States
Troutdale, OR
10/12/2024